Don't Get Played:

Your Guide to Outsmarting Manipulators

Index:

Introduction

Manipulation and deceptive persuasion are not limited to fiction or high-stakes situations. In reality, they're woven into the fabric of our daily lives—used in subtle ways by individuals, institutions, and businesses. We encounter manipulation in relationships, the workplace, and even the advertisements we see. Often, we aren't aware of the ways we're being influenced, but the impact is real.

This book is a practical guide for recognizing and countering manipulation, equipping you with knowledge to navigate social and professional environments confidently. From understanding the psychology behind manipulation to developing the skills to defend yourself, the goal is to help you avoid becoming a victim of manipulation, taking control of your interactions, and ensuring they remain authentic and fair.

Part 1: Understanding Manipulation and Persuasion

Chapter 1: The Psychology of Manipulation

Manipulation is rooted in psychological principles that have been studied for decades. Whether it's the use of cognitive biases, emotional triggers, or social conditioning, manipulators rely on predictable patterns in human thinking and behavior. This chapter will explore the foundations of manipulation, including the psychological mechanisms that make people susceptible, such as the power of authority, social proof, and reciprocity.

Cognitive Biases and How They Affect Decision-Making

Cognitive biases are mental shortcuts, or heuristics, that our brains use to process information quickly and efficiently. While these shortcuts are essential for handling the vast amount of data we encounter every day, they can also lead to systematic errors in thinking. These errors—known as cognitive biases—affect our perceptions, decisions, and judgments, often without us realizing it.

Manipulators are adept at exploiting cognitive biases to influence others. By understanding how these biases work, we can become more aware of our own decision-making processes and guard against manipulation.

1. Confirmation Bias

Confirmation bias refers to the tendency to search for, interpret, and remember information that confirms our preexisting beliefs, while ignoring or downplaying information that contradicts them. This bias reinforces what we already think is true, making it difficult to approach situations with an open mind.

Manipulators take advantage of confirmation bias by feeding us information that aligns with our existing beliefs. In sales, for example, a salesperson may emphasize features of a product that match our preferences while downplaying any drawbacks. In relationships, manipulators may echo our values and opinions to gain our trust, even if their true beliefs are different. Once they've established this trust, they can slowly introduce more manipulative tactics without raising suspicion.

How to Defend Yourself: To counter confirmation bias, practice critical thinking and seek out opposing viewpoints. Challenge your assumptions by asking, "What evidence would prove me wrong?" Deliberately exposing yourself to alternative perspectives can help you make more balanced, informed decisions.

2. Anchoring Bias

Anchoring bias occurs when we rely too heavily on the first piece of information we receive (the "anchor") when making decisions. This initial information serves as a reference point, influencing how we interpret subsequent data. Even if the anchor is irrelevant or misleading, it can skew our judgment.

In negotiations, for instance, an initial offer often serves as an anchor, setting the tone for the rest of the discussion. If a manipulator proposes an unreasonably high price, it can make a slightly lower—but still inflated—price seem reasonable by comparison. Similarly, in conversations, a manipulator might frame their requests in such a way that the first suggestion sets a precedent, making any subsequent demands seem less excessive.

How to Defend Yourself: Be aware of the anchoring effect by taking a step back before making decisions. Consider all available information and resist the temptation to focus solely on the first data point you encounter. Delaying judgment until you've explored alternative perspectives can help neutralize the influence of anchors.

3. Availability Heuristic

The availability heuristic is the tendency to judge the likelihood of an event based on how easily examples come to mind. If we can quickly recall an example of something happening, we are more likely to believe that it is common or likely to occur. This bias is often influenced by media coverage, personal experiences, and vivid stories.

Manipulators use the availability heuristic by highlighting dramatic or emotionally charged examples to sway our thinking. For instance, a politician might focus on a sensational crime story to convince voters that crime is on the rise, even if overall statistics show a decline. In personal relationships, a manipulative partner may repeatedly bring up past mistakes to make you feel like you're prone to failure, even if those mistakes were rare.

How to Defend Yourself: To combat the availability heuristic, seek out objective data and broader trends rather than relying solely on anecdotes or isolated examples. Ask yourself whether the information presented is representative of the larger picture, and whether emotionally charged examples are being used to cloud your judgment.

4. Loss Aversion

Loss aversion refers to the fact that people tend to fear losses more than they value gains. In other words, the pain of losing something is often stronger than the pleasure of gaining something of equal value. This bias can lead to irrational decision-making, as we might go to great lengths to avoid loss, even when it's not in our best interest.

Manipulators exploit loss aversion by framing situations in terms of what you stand to lose rather than what you stand to gain. For example, a manipulative employer might imply that turning down extra work will jeopardize your job security, even if taking on the extra work comes at the cost of your health or personal life. In relationships, a manipulative partner might use threats of abandonment to make you stay in an unhealthy situation out of fear of losing the relationship.

How to Defend Yourself: Recognize when decisions are being framed in terms of losses and take a step back to consider the bigger picture. Ask yourself whether the fear of loss is clouding your judgment and whether the proposed loss is truly significant. Evaluating decisions from a neutral perspective—focusing on both potential losses and gains—can help you make more rational choices.

Emotional Vulnerability and Psychological Triggers

Emotions play a powerful role in human behavior, and manipulators know how to exploit emotional vulnerabilities to achieve their goals. By triggering certain emotional responses, they can gain control over our actions and decisions. Understanding these psychological triggers is key to defending ourselves against emotional manipulation.

1. Fear

Fear is one of the most primal and powerful emotions. It can override logic, compelling us to act impulsively to avoid perceived danger. Manipulators often use fear to create a sense of urgency or helplessness, pushing us to make decisions we might not otherwise consider.

In political campaigns, fear is often used to sway voters by emphasizing threats to safety or stability. In relationships, a manipulative partner might create a fear of abandonment or rejection to keep you dependent on them. By instilling fear, manipulators can force you into a reactive state where you're more focused on avoiding danger than making rational choices.

How to Defend Yourself: To counter fear-based manipulation, take a moment to assess the situation logically. Ask yourself whether the threat is real and immediate, or whether it's being exaggerated. Slow down your decision-making process to avoid making choices based on fear alone. Seeking a second opinion from someone you trust can also help provide perspective.

2. Guilt

Guilt is another emotion that manipulators frequently exploit. By making you feel responsible for their well-being or happiness, they can control your actions through guilt-tripping. This is particularly effective in close relationships, where emotional ties are strong.

For example, a manipulative family member might remind you of sacrifices they've made for you, implying that you owe them something in return. A partner might use guilt to prevent you from setting boundaries, making you feel selfish for prioritizing your own needs. Over time, guilt can erode your sense of self-worth, making you more susceptible to further manipulation.

How to Defend Yourself: To avoid falling into guilt traps, recognize when someone is attempting to make you responsible for their feelings or actions. It's important to remember that you are not obligated to meet unreasonable demands, especially if they come at the expense of your well-being. Establishing healthy boundaries and practicing self-compassion can help you resist guilt-based manipulation.

3. Flattery and Ingratiation

While fear and guilt are negative emotions, positive emotions like pride and self-esteem can also be manipulated. Flattery and ingratiation—where someone excessively praises or compliments you—can be used to lower your defenses and make you more compliant.

A manipulative colleague, for instance, might shower you with praise before asking for a favor, knowing that you'll be more likely to say yes if you feel appreciated. In relationships, manipulators might use love bombing—a tactic where they overwhelm you with affection early on—to create a sense of dependence, making it harder to see their ulterior motives later.

How to Defend Yourself: Be cautious of excessive or insincere praise. While it's natural to enjoy compliments, consider whether the flattery is being used to manipulate your actions. Healthy relationships are built on mutual respect and appreciation, not manipulation through praise. Pay attention to whether the praise is followed by a request or expectation, and don't feel obligated to reciprocate out of a sense of indebtedness.

4. Sympathy and Pity

Manipulators often play the victim to evoke sympathy and manipulate your emotions. By portraying themselves as helpless or in need, they can make you feel obligated to help them, even when it's not in your best interest. This is especially common in toxic relationships, where the manipulator uses their perceived vulnerability to maintain control.

For example, a manipulative friend might constantly share stories of personal hardship, subtly implying that you should prioritize their needs over your own. In more extreme cases, abusers may use sympathy to keep their victims from leaving, claiming that they "can't survive" without them.

How to Defend Yourself: Recognize when someone is using their hardships as a means of control. While it's important to be compassionate, it's equally important to set boundaries and prioritize your well-being. Not every request for help is genuine, and you are not obligated to sacrifice your needs for someone who consistently plays the victim.

The Role of Power Dynamics in Manipulation

Power dynamics play a critical role in manipulation, as those with more power—whether it's social, economic, or emotional—can more easily influence and control others. Understanding these dynamics is essential to recognizing when manipulation is at play.

1. Authority

The authority bias is the tendency to follow the instructions or opinions of someone in a position of authority, even when it may not be in our best interest. This bias is deeply ingrained in human behavior, as we are conditioned to respect and defer to authority figures, whether they are teachers, bosses, or experts.

Manipulators in positions of authority can exploit this bias by leveraging their status to push you into compliance. For instance, a boss might use their authority to pressure you into working overtime, knowing that you're unlikely to challenge them due to the power imbalance. In relationships, a partner who controls financial resources or decision-making power may use this leverage to maintain control.

How to Defend Yourself: Question authority when necessary. While it's important to respect legitimate authority, it's equally important to recognize when it's being used to manipulate or control. Ask yourself whether the person's position of power justifies their requests, and don't be afraid to push back if you feel uncomfortable or coerced.

2. Dependency

In relationships where there is a significant power imbalance, dependency becomes a key factor in manipulation. If one person relies on the other for financial support, emotional validation, or social status, the more powerful individual can use this dependency to maintain control.

For example, in an abusive relationship, a manipulative partner might isolate the victim from friends and family, making them more dependent on the abuser for support and validation. This creates a power imbalance where the victim feels trapped and unable to leave, even when the relationship is harmful.

How to Defend Yourself: Building independence is crucial in avoiding manipulation. This might involve gaining financial independence, strengthening your support network, or developing emotional resilience. By reducing your dependence on others, you can maintain more control over your own decisions and avoid being manipulated through dependency.

3. Social Status and Reputation

Social hierarchies and reputations can also be used as tools for manipulation. Individuals with higher social status—whether due to wealth, popularity, or influence—may use their position to manipulate those with less power. This can manifest in subtle ways, such as using charm or charisma to gain favors, or in more overt ways, such as leveraging social connections to coerce or intimidate.

In professional settings, a well-connected colleague might use their social capital to pressure you into agreeing with their ideas, knowing that disagreeing could damage your reputation. In relationships, a manipulative partner may use public humiliation or social exclusion as a means of control.

How to Defend Yourself: Be aware of how social status and reputation are being used in your interactions. While it's natural to respect those with influence, don't let their status overshadow your judgment or values. Maintain your integrity, and don't allow the fear of social consequences to dictate your actions.

By understanding how cognitive biases, emotional triggers, and power dynamics contribute to manipulation, you can become more aware of when you are being influenced. Developing critical thinking skills, emotional resilience, and the ability to recognize power imbalances can help you navigate social interactions with greater confidence and control. The more you understand these dynamics, the better equipped you will be to protect yourself from manipulation in all areas of life.

Chapter 2: The Art of Persuasion

Persuasion, when used ethically, can be a valuable communication tool. However, in the hands of a manipulator, it becomes a weapon. This chapter explores the differences between healthy persuasion and manipulative tactics. We'll delve into strategies such as ingratiation, the foot-in-the-door technique, and emotional appeals that push people to act against their better judgment.

Persuasion vs. Manipulation

At first glance, persuasion and manipulation may seem like two sides of the same coin. Both involve influencing others to achieve a desired outcome. However, the key difference lies in intent and ethics. Persuasion is a process of influencing others in an open, transparent way, where both parties understand the nature of the interaction. It respects the autonomy and free will of the person being persuaded. In contrast, manipulation is deceitful and covert, intending to control or coerce someone into a decision that may not be in their best interest.

The Ethics of Influence

Persuasion, when used ethically, aims to present facts, emotions, or arguments in a way that aligns with the audience's needs, values, or desires. The persuader may encourage the other person to take a certain action, but the final choice is left up to the individual. The use of persuasion respects the individual's autonomy and ability to weigh options before making a decision.

For example, a health professional may use persuasion to encourage patients to adopt healthier lifestyles, presenting the benefits of diet and exercise in a factual, motivational way. Here, persuasion is used to benefit the individual, aligning their actions with long-term well-being.

Manipulation, however, operates with hidden motives. It involves the use of psychological tricks, deceit, and emotional exploitation to steer someone toward a decision they may not fully understand or would not willingly choose if they were fully informed. Manipulators often withhold key information, present false choices, or pressure people emotionally.

Take, for instance, a salesperson using manipulation to pressure a customer into buying a product by falsely suggesting that the offer will expire soon, even though there is no real time limit. Here, the manipulator exploits the fear of missing out to rush the customer into a purchase they might regret later.

Transparency vs. Deception

Another critical distinction between persuasion and manipulation is the level of transparency. Ethical persuasion involves clear communication. The person being persuaded knows what's being asked of them and why. Persuaders provide information, allowing the individual to make a well-informed decision.

In contrast, manipulation thrives on deception. Manipulators often mislead others, either through outright lies or by withholding critical information. For example, a manipulator in a relationship may give their partner false reassurances while secretly pursuing other goals, creating an environment of mistrust and control.

How to Defend Yourself: The key to defending against manipulation is to be mindful of the level of transparency in any interaction. Ask yourself: Is the other person being honest and clear about their intentions? Are they providing all the information I need to make an informed decision? If you feel rushed, pressured, or like you're not getting the full picture, it could be a sign of manipulation.

Tactics like Ingratiation, Reciprocity, and Authority Influence

Influence tactics are often used to sway decisions, whether for ethical persuasion or more sinister manipulation. Some of the most common tactics include ingratiation, reciprocity, and authority influence. Understanding these tactics helps you recognize when they are being used and whether they are part of a healthy interaction or manipulative scheme.

Ingratiation: The Power of Flattery

Ingratiation involves using flattery, praise, or other forms of positive reinforcement to make someone more favorable toward a request. The person being influenced feels good about themselves and, in turn, becomes more likely to comply with the influencer's desires. While flattery can be sincere and well-intentioned in some cases, ingratiation becomes manipulative when the praise is disingenuous or used solely to manipulate emotions for personal gain.

For example, in the workplace, a colleague may shower their boss with compliments, hoping to secure a promotion or favorable treatment. In relationships, ingratiation might involve excessive praise or attention at the beginning of a romance (often referred to as "love bombing"), creating an emotional bond that makes the recipient more susceptible to control later.

Manipulators use ingratiation to make their targets feel indebted or obligated to reciprocate the goodwill. Once the person being flattered feels emotionally connected, they may be more likely to comply with future requests, even when those requests are unreasonable or not in their best interest.

How to Defend Yourself: Be cautious when faced with excessive or insincere praise. Ask yourself whether the flattery seems genuine or if it's part of a larger strategy to win your favor. Take a step back and evaluate whether you're being asked to do something in return, and whether that request aligns with your values or best interests.

Reciprocity: The Obligation to Return Favors

Reciprocity is a powerful social norm that obligates individuals to return a favor when someone does something for them. It's deeply ingrained in human culture and essential for fostering cooperation and social bonds. However, manipulators exploit this principle by giving something small or superficial, knowing that the recipient will feel compelled to reciprocate, often with something much larger.

For instance, in marketing, companies may offer free samples or gifts, creating a sense of obligation in the consumer to make a purchase. In social relationships, a manipulative person might perform small favors or acts of kindness, later using those as leverage to ask for something far more significant.

Reciprocity works because it triggers a sense of indebtedness, which can override rational decision-making. People want to avoid feeling like they're "in debt" to someone, and this discomfort can push them to make decisions they wouldn't otherwise consider.

How to Defend Yourself: Recognize when someone is using reciprocity to manipulate you. While it's normal to want to return favors, consider whether the favor you're being asked for is proportional to what was given to you. If the original favor was unsolicited or trivial, you are not obligated to return it with something more valuable. Practice saying no, and remind yourself that manipulation often involves creating false obligations.

Authority Influence: Trusting the Experts

The authority principle refers to our tendency to comply with requests or follow instructions from individuals in positions of authority or expertise.

This influence tactic is rooted in the belief that authority figures—such as doctors, lawyers, or leaders—possess superior knowledge, making their guidance valuable. While this can be a positive force in society, authority influence becomes manipulative when the authority figure is untrustworthy, deceptive, or uses their status to exploit others.

For example, a manipulative boss may use their position to pressure employees into working overtime without additional pay, suggesting that questioning their authority will harm their career. In marketing, companies might use endorsements from perceived experts to sell products, even when the endorsements are exaggerated or misleading.

The power of authority influence comes from our deeply ingrained respect for knowledge and status. When someone we perceive as an expert provides guidance, we often accept it without critically analyzing the information ourselves.

How to Defend Yourself: Challenge authority when necessary by asking questions and seeking independent verification of the information being presented. Just because someone holds a position of power or expertise doesn't mean they are always acting in your best interest. It's important to balance respect for authority with critical thinking and a willingness to push back when something feels wrong.

How Emotions Are Used to Steer Decisions

Emotions are central to human decision-making. While logical reasoning plays a role in many of our choices, emotions often drive our actions, especially when decisions are made quickly or under pressure. Manipulators are skilled at using emotions to steer decisions, knowing that emotional appeals can bypass logical thinking and create a sense of urgency, connection, or fear that leads to compliance.

Fear: The Ultimate Motivator

Fear is one of the most powerful emotions a manipulator can trigger. Fear-based manipulation works by creating a sense of urgency, danger, or impending loss that compels the individual to act immediately, often without fully considering their options.

For example, a scammer might send a fraudulent email claiming that your bank account has been compromised and urging you to click on a link to secure it. The fear of losing your money overrides your normal caution, leading you to act impulsively. Similarly, in relationships, a manipulative partner might use fear tactics such as threats of abandonment or emotional withdrawal to keep you from setting boundaries or making independent decisions.

Fear manipulates us by narrowing our focus. When we're afraid, we become hyper-focused on avoiding the threat, often at the expense of evaluating alternative solutions or considering long-term consequences.

How to Defend Yourself: Recognize when fear is being used to manipulate you. Take a step back and assess whether the threat is real or exaggerated. Whenever possible, delay making decisions in fear-driven situations, giving yourself time to think rationally. Seek advice from a trusted third party who can offer perspective.

Guilt and Obligation: Emotional Blackmail

Guilt is another emotion commonly used to manipulate decisions. Emotional manipulators play on your sense of responsibility or morality, making you feel guilty for not meeting their needs or expectations. This guilt can push you to act against your better judgment, doing things you wouldn't otherwise agree to out of a desire to relieve the emotional pressure.

In relationships, guilt might be used in the form of emotional blackmail, where a partner makes you feel responsible for their happiness or well-being. They may say things like, "If you really loved me, you'd do this for me," or, "I've done so much for you; how could you refuse me this?" By framing the situation in moral or emotional terms, they make it difficult for you to say no without feeling like a bad person.

Guilt manipulates us by exploiting our desire to be good, compassionate, and responsible. When someone uses guilt against us, it distorts our moral compass, making us feel obligated to act in ways that don't align with our true values.

How to Defend Yourself: When someone tries to manipulate you with guilt, take a moment to separate your feelings from your obligations. Remind yourself that you are not responsible for other people's emotions, and that you have the right to prioritize your own needs and boundaries.

Practice assertiveness by saying no without feeling compelled to justify your decision.

Love and Affection: Creating Emotional Dependency

Love is one of the most profound emotions, and when used genuinely, it can form the foundation for strong, healthy relationships. However, manipulative individuals may use love, affection, or the promise of intimacy as tools to create emotional dependency. This tactic is often seen in relationships where one partner uses emotional closeness as leverage to control the other.

For instance, a manipulative person might withhold affection or approval to punish their partner, knowing that the fear of losing love will drive compliance. In other cases, they may shower the person with affection at key moments (as seen in the tactic of love bombing), creating an intense emotional bond that makes it difficult for the victim to recognize red flags or leave the relationship.

Emotional dependency is powerful because it taps into our deep human need for connection, love, and belonging. When love is used as a manipulation tool, it can distort our perception of the relationship, making us more vulnerable to control.

How to Defend Yourself: Recognize the signs of emotional manipulation in relationships. If affection or love is being used as a reward or punishment, it's a red flag that the relationship may not be healthy. Ensure that your emotional needs are being met on an equal, mutual basis, and don't be afraid to step away from relationships that feel manipulative or controlling.

By understanding the difference between persuasion and manipulation, recognizing influence tactics, and knowing how emotions are used to steer decisions, you can build greater awareness of when you are being influenced. Critical thinking, emotional intelligence, and assertiveness are your best defenses against manipulation in all areas of life.

Chapter 3: Body Language and Microexpressions

Often, manipulation occurs not through words, but through non-verbal cues—subtle gestures, facial expressions, and body language. Understanding how to read and interpret these signs is critical in detecting hidden agendas. This chapter will introduce the basics of body language analysis and teach you how to recognize common microexpressions that reveal deception or hidden intentions.

Body language is a fundamental form of non-verbal communication. While we often focus on words when interacting with others, much of what we communicate is transmitted through our posture, gestures, facial expressions, and other subtle cues. These non-verbal signals can reveal underlying emotions and intentions that may not be spoken aloud, and understanding them can help us navigate social interactions with greater insight.

In this chapter, we'll explore the basics of reading body language, the role of microexpressions in conveying emotions, and the specific signs that indicate discomfort, evasion, or dishonesty. By honing your ability to read these cues, you'll gain a deeper understanding of people's true feelings, even when their words may be misleading.

The Basics of Reading Body Language

Body language involves a wide range of physical behaviors that, consciously or unconsciously, communicate feelings, thoughts, and intentions. These signals can be as subtle as a slight change in posture or as obvious as a broad smile. Learning to read body language allows you to tap into the unspoken elements of communication.

Open vs. Closed Body Language

One of the most fundamental distinctions in body language is between "open" and "closed" postures. Open body language signals comfort, confidence, and receptivity, while closed body language can indicate discomfort, defensiveness, or a desire to distance oneself.

Open Body Language:

- Relaxed posture: When someone is at ease, their body will be more relaxed, with their arms and legs uncrossed. They may lean slightly forward, showing interest in the conversation.
- Palms visible: Open palms are a universal sign of honesty and openness. When people display their palms, they're often signaling that they have nothing to hide.
- Feet pointing toward you: Feet are often overlooked in body language, but they can be quite telling. If someone's feet are pointed toward you, it usually indicates that they are engaged and interested in the interaction.

Closed Body Language:

- Crossed arms or legs: When someone crosses their arms or legs, it often signals defensiveness or discomfort. This can be a subconscious attempt to create a barrier between themselves and others, indicating that they feel threatened or want to protect themselves.

- Leaning away: A person who leans away from you may be distancing themselves, either emotionally or physically. This can suggest disinterest, discomfort, or even distrust.

- Feet pointing away: When someone's feet are pointed away from you, it can be a sign that they are disengaged or looking for an escape from the conversation.

Posture and Confidence

The way someone carries themselves can reveal a great deal about their confidence level. Confident individuals tend to stand or sit with their shoulders back, head held high, and spine straight. This "powerful" posture suggests that they feel comfortable in their environment and in control of the situation.

Conversely, someone who is feeling insecure or unsure may slouch, hunch their shoulders, or shrink into themselves, as if trying to take up less space. This posture can indicate nervousness, fear, or submission.

How to Read Confidence:

- Strong posture: Upright posture, with shoulders back and head level, often signals confidence. Confident people are also more likely to make direct eye contact and use expansive gestures.
- Hunched or slouched posture: A hunched posture or shoulders that are drawn inward can signal discomfort, insecurity, or a lack of confidence. This is especially common in social situations where someone feels out of place or nervous.

Gestures and Movement

Gestures, particularly hand movements, are an essential part of body language. People often use their hands to emphasize points, convey emotions, or illustrate ideas. However, gestures can also be involuntary, revealing hidden thoughts or emotions.

Illustrative Gestures:

- Talking with hands: When people use their hands to "talk," gesturing as they speak, it can indicate enthusiasm, energy, and confidence. This type of body language is often seen in people who are passionate about what they're saying.
- Fidgeting: On the other hand, fidgeting—such as tapping fingers, playing with hair, or bouncing a leg—can signal nervousness, impatience, or discomfort. Fidgeting may indicate that the person is feeling anxious or restless.

How to Read Gestures:

- Mirroring: When two people are comfortable and in sync with each other, they often unconsciously mirror each other's body language. If someone mirrors your posture, gestures, or expressions, it's a good sign that they are engaged and building rapport with you.

- Inconsistent gestures: When someone's gestures don't align with their words, it can be a sign of dishonesty or discomfort. For example, if someone says they're excited but their body language is stiff or closed off, it's worth paying attention to the discrepancy.

Facial Expressions: The Window to Emotion

Facial expressions are perhaps the most obvious and immediate form of non-verbal communication. We use our faces to express a wide range of emotions, often without even realizing it. While some facial expressions are universal (such as smiling to show happiness), others can be more subtle and context-dependent.

Key Facial Expressions to Watch:

- Smiles: A genuine smile involves not just the mouth, but also the eyes, which crinkle at the corners. A fake or forced smile may only engage the mouth, leaving the eyes unchanged.
- Furrowed brow: A furrowed brow can indicate confusion, concentration, or concern. It's often a sign that someone is thinking hard or trying to work through a problem.
- Eye contact: Eye contact is one of the most powerful forms of non-verbal communication. Direct eye contact can signal confidence, interest, and honesty, while avoiding eye contact may indicate discomfort, shyness, or deceit.

By learning to interpret these basic elements of body language, you can gain valuable insight into people's emotions and intentions. However, body language is not always straightforward—sometimes, the most telling signals are the fleeting microexpressions that flit across someone's face in a fraction of a second.

Microexpressions and Their Connection to Emotions

Microexpressions are brief, involuntary facial expressions that occur when someone is trying to conceal or suppress their true feelings. These tiny flashes of emotion can last as little as a fraction of a second, but they provide a window into what a person is really feeling beneath the surface. Because microexpressions are so fleeting, they often go unnoticed by those who aren't trained to look for them.

The Science of Microexpressions

Microexpressions were first studied in detail by psychologist Paul Ekman, who identified seven universal facial expressions that are linked to specific emotions. These emotions are happiness, sadness, anger, fear, surprise, disgust, and contempt. No matter what culture or background a person comes from, these basic emotions are expressed in the same way.

For example, when someone feels disgust, their nose may wrinkle, and their upper lip may curl. When someone feels fear, their eyes widen, and their eyebrows rise. These expressions are universal because they are hardwired into the human brain, and they occur involuntarily—even when someone is trying to hide their emotions.

How to Spot Microexpressions:

- Watch the eyes: The eyes are particularly expressive and often reveal emotions that people try to hide. When someone is angry, their eyes may narrow, and their eyebrows may draw together. When someone is afraid, their eyes may widen, and their pupils may dilate.

- Look for fleeting changes: Microexpressions are incredibly brief, lasting only a fraction of a second. However, with practice, you can learn to catch these fleeting changes in someone's face. For example, you might notice a quick flash of anger in someone's eyes before they compose themselves and put on a neutral expression.

- Focus on the mouth and eyebrows: In addition to the eyes, the mouth and eyebrows are key areas to watch for microexpressions. A slight tightening of the lips can indicate anger or frustration, while raised eyebrows can signal surprise or fear.

The Role of Microexpressions in Detecting Deception

Microexpressions are particularly useful in detecting deception because they often reveal emotions that someone is trying to hide. For example, if someone is lying, they may try to maintain a calm, neutral expression, but a flash of fear or guilt may briefly cross their face. Similarly, someone who is pretending to be happy may struggle to conceal a momentary expression of sadness or frustration.

Because microexpressions are involuntary, they are difficult to control or suppress. This makes them a valuable tool for spotting lies or hidden emotions.

How to Use Microexpressions to Detect Lies:

- Look for incongruent emotions: When someone's facial expressions don't match their words, it's a sign that they may be hiding something. For example, if someone says they're happy but their face briefly flashes with sadness, they may not be telling the full truth.

- Pay attention to timing: Microexpressions often occur before someone has a chance to compose themselves. If you notice a fleeting expression of anger or fear before someone puts on a neutral face, it's a clue that their initial reaction was more emotional than they're letting on.

- Combine microexpressions with other cues: While microexpressions are a powerful tool, they should be used in conjunction with other body language and verbal cues to get a complete picture of someone's emotions. For example, if someone's body language is closed off and they're fidgeting while showing microexpressions of discomfort, it's a strong indicator that they're feeling anxious or deceptive.

Signs of Discomfort, Evasion, or Dishonesty

When someone is uncomfortable, evasive, or dishonest, their body language and microexpressions can provide subtle but telling clues. These cues often reveal more than words alone and can help you identify when someone is being deceptive or withholding information.

Signs of Discomfort

Discomfort can manifest in many ways, from nervous fidgeting to avoiding eye contact. People who are uncomfortable may also exhibit physical tension, such as clenching their fists or tightening their jaw.

Common Signs of Discomfort:

- Fidgeting: Restless movements, such as tapping fingers, bouncing a leg, or adjusting clothing, can indicate nervousness or discomfort. These behaviors are often attempts to release pent-up energy or anxiety.

- Avoiding eye contact: When someone feels uncomfortable or guilty, they may avoid making direct eye contact. This can be a subconscious attempt to distance themselves from the situation or to avoid revealing their true emotions.

- Tense body language: Physical tension, such as clenched fists, a stiff posture, or tight facial muscles, can signal discomfort. This is especially common in situations where someone feels threatened or defensive.

Signs of Evasion

Evasive behavior often involves avoiding direct answers, deflecting questions, or using vague language. People who are being evasive may also use body language to create physical distance, such as leaning away or turning their body slightly away from the person they're speaking to.

Common Signs of Evasion:

- Vague answers: If someone is avoiding a question, they may give non-specific or overly general answers. They may also repeat the question or try to change the subject.

- Shifting body language: People who are being evasive may physically distance themselves by leaning away, crossing their arms, or turning their body away. These behaviors can indicate a desire to escape the conversation or avoid scrutiny.

- Hesitation: Evasive individuals may hesitate before answering questions, as they try to come up with a response that avoids revealing too much information.

Signs of Dishonesty

Dishonesty can be difficult to detect, but certain body language cues and microexpressions can reveal when someone is lying. In addition to avoiding eye contact and fidgeting, liars may display microexpressions of guilt, fear, or anxiety.

Common Signs of Dishonesty:

- Inconsistent body language: When someone's body language doesn't match their words, it's often a sign of dishonesty. For example, if someone says they're confident but their body is closed off and tense, they may not be telling the truth.

- Microexpressions of guilt or fear: Liars may briefly show signs of guilt or fear before they regain control of their facial expressions. These microexpressions can include furrowed brows, tightened lips, or widened eyes.

- Overcompensation: Sometimes, liars will go out of their way to appear honest, offering more details than necessary or using exaggerated body language to convince others of their sincerity. This can be a red flag that they are trying too hard to appear truthful.

By learning to read body language and microexpressions, you can gain valuable insight into the emotions and intentions of those around you. Whether someone is feeling confident, uncomfortable, evasive, or dishonest, their non-verbal cues can provide important clues that help you navigate social interactions more effectively.

Part 2: Manipulation in Everyday Life

Chapter 4: Manipulation in Relationships

Personal relationships are one of the most common arenas for manipulation. Whether it's romantic partners, friends, or family members, emotional manipulation can be subtle but powerful. This chapter will explore tactics such as gaslighting, guilt-tripping, and emotional blackmail, helping you identify when someone close to you is trying to control your emotions or actions.

Relationships can be among the most rewarding and fulfilling parts of life, but they can also be fraught with challenges, especially when manipulation is involved. Emotional manipulation is a particularly insidious form of control, often used by individuals to gain power over their partners, friends, or family members. This chapter will delve into various forms of manipulation that occur in relationships, such as emotional manipulation and gaslighting, the dynamics created by power imbalances, and how to recognize and respond to toxic relationships.

Emotional Manipulation and Gaslighting

Emotional manipulation is a form of psychological abuse where one person uses deceptive, unfair, or coercive tactics to control or influence another person's emotions and behavior. Unlike direct physical abuse, emotional manipulation is often subtle and difficult to detect, leaving the victim doubting their perceptions or questioning their self-worth.

What is Emotional Manipulation?

Emotional manipulation involves influencing someone's feelings and perceptions for personal gain. It can take many forms, ranging from guilt trips to feigned victimhood to more calculated strategies like gaslighting. Manipulative people often target a person's emotional vulnerabilities, using those weak points as leverage to achieve their own ends.

Common Emotional Manipulation Tactics:

- Guilt Tripping: Manipulators often exploit their victim's sense of responsibility or empathy, making them feel guilty for things that are not their fault. This might sound like, "After everything I've done for you, how could you even think that?" or "You're the only one who can make this right."
- Withholding Affection or Approval: A manipulator may withdraw love, affection, or approval as a way to punish their partner or get them to comply. This could manifest in silent treatment, avoiding physical touch, or giving backhanded compliments to undermine the victim's self-esteem.
- Playing the Victim: Many manipulators use victimhood as a tool. They exaggerate or fabricate hardships to gain sympathy or deflect responsibility. This tactic forces their partner to focus on their needs, rather than addressing legitimate concerns or conflicts in the relationship.

- Gaslighting: One of the most damaging forms of emotional manipulation, gaslighting, is a technique in which the manipulator makes the victim doubt their own memory, perception, or sanity. Over time, this can erode the victim's confidence in their judgment and increase their reliance on the manipulator.

Understanding Gaslighting

Gaslighting is a particularly destructive form of manipulation, as it undermines the victim's sense of reality. The term originates from the 1944 film Gaslight, in which a man manipulates his wife into doubting her perception of events by gradually dimming the gaslights in their home and then denying that the lighting has changed. Over time, the wife begins to question her sanity.

How Gaslighting Works:

- Denial of Reality: A gaslighter will blatantly deny that certain events occurred, even when presented with evidence to the contrary. This might involve statements like, "That never happened," or "You're just imagining things." Over time, the victim begins to question their memory and perception of reality.

- Minimization: Gaslighters will often downplay their actions, telling the victim they are overreacting or being too sensitive. They may say, "You're making a big deal out of nothing," or "You're just being dramatic," which leads the victim to second-guess their feelings.

- Projection: Gaslighters often accuse the victim of the very behavior they are guilty of. For example, a partner who is lying or being unfaithful may accuse the victim of dishonesty or cheating. This tactic distracts from the manipulator's behavior while placing the victim on the defensive.

- Isolation: Gaslighters frequently work to isolate their victims from friends, family, or any outside influences that might help the victim see the truth. By limiting the victim's support network, the gaslighter makes it harder for them to gain perspective or escape the toxic relationship.

The Psychological Impact of Gaslighting: Over time, gaslighting can severely damage a person's mental health. Victims may experience confusion, anxiety, depression, and a growing sense of self-doubt. Because gaslighting distorts the victim's perception of reality, they may become increasingly reliant on the manipulator for guidance, believing they are incapable of making decisions on their own.

Power Imbalances in Relationships

Power imbalances are at the heart of many manipulative relationships. In a healthy relationship, both partners share power equally, with each person having an equal say in decisions and mutual respect for one another's boundaries. However, in a manipulative relationship, one partner may exert control over the other, creating an unhealthy dynamic where one person has significantly more power.

What Creates a Power Imbalance?

Power imbalances can be caused by many factors, including financial dependency, emotional vulnerability, differences in social status, or even personality traits. Often, the manipulator seeks to amplify these imbalances to maintain control.

Factors Contributing to Power Imbalances:

1. Financial Dependency: If one partner is financially dependent on the other, they may feel trapped in the relationship because they lack the resources to leave. Manipulators often exploit this by withholding money,

controlling financial decisions, or using money as a tool to reward or punish.

2. Emotional Dependency: Emotional dependency occurs when one partner relies heavily on the other for validation, self-esteem, or a sense of purpose. Manipulators may exploit their partner's need for love or approval by making them feel unworthy or inadequate unless they comply with the manipulator's demands.

3. Social or Cultural Norms: In some cases, cultural or societal norms may contribute to power imbalances. For example, in some cultures, traditional gender roles may place one partner in a position of dominance, making it easier for them to exert control over the other.

4. Personality Traits: Narcissistic or controlling individuals are more likely to create power imbalances in relationships. They may use charm, manipulation, or intimidation to assert dominance and keep their partner in a subservient role.

The Impact of Power Imbalances

When there is a power imbalance in a relationship, the dominant partner often uses manipulation, control, and coercion to maintain their position. The partner with less power may feel voiceless, helpless, or unable to advocate for themselves. Over time, this imbalance can lead to emotional abuse, as the dominant partner exploits their power to control the other person's behavior, decisions, and even thoughts.

Signs of a Power Imbalance:

- One partner makes all the decisions: In a healthy relationship, decisions are made collaboratively. However, in a relationship with a power imbalance, one partner often takes control, making decisions about finances, social activities, and even personal matters without consulting the other.

- One partner dominates conversations: In a relationship with a power imbalance, the dominant partner may control conversations, dismiss the other's opinions, or speak for them. The less powerful partner may feel that their voice doesn't matter or that their thoughts are not valued.

- Fear of retaliation: If one partner fears retaliation or punishment for speaking up or disagreeing, this is a clear sign of a power imbalance. The dominant partner may use threats, guilt, or emotional manipulation to keep the other partner compliant.

- One partner controls resources: A manipulative partner may control access to resources such as money, transportation, or even social connections. This control is used to maintain dominance and keep the other partner dependent.

Addressing Power Imbalances

Recognizing a power imbalance is the first step toward addressing it. It's important to have open and honest conversations about the dynamic in the relationship and work together to restore balance.

However, if one partner is unwilling to acknowledge the imbalance or work toward equality, the relationship may be inherently toxic and unhealthy.

Steps to Address a Power Imbalance:

1. Open Communication: Begin by discussing the power dynamics in the relationship openly and without judgment. A healthy partner will be willing to listen and make changes to ensure both partners have an equal say.

2. Establish Boundaries: Boundaries are essential in restoring balance to a relationship. Both partners should have clear boundaries that respect their autonomy, and these boundaries must be honored.

3. Seek Professional Help: In cases where power imbalances are deeply ingrained, couples counseling or individual therapy may be necessary to address underlying issues and rebuild a healthier dynamic.

4. Build Independence: For the less powerful partner, building financial, emotional, and social independence can help restore balance in the relationship. This might involve pursuing a career, building a support network, or developing new hobbies and interests outside the relationship.

Recognizing and Responding to Toxic Dynamics

Toxic relationships are characterized by unhealthy patterns of behavior, manipulation, and emotional abuse. These relationships can drain your energy, self-esteem, and emotional well-being, making it difficult to maintain a sense of personal autonomy. Recognizing the signs of toxic dynamics is critical for protecting yourself from further harm.

Recognizing Toxic Relationship Dynamics

Toxic relationships often follow predictable patterns of behavior. Manipulators use various tactics to maintain control over their partner, ranging from emotional abuse to gaslighting to constant criticism. Over time, these behaviors can erode the victim's sense of self-worth and make it difficult to leave the relationship.

Common Signs of Toxic Dynamics:

- Constant Criticism: In a toxic relationship, one partner frequently criticizes or belittles the other, often under the guise of "helping" or "improving" them. This constant criticism can damage the victim's self-esteem and make them feel as though they are never good enough.
- Emotional Rollercoaster: Toxic relationships are often characterized by extreme highs and lows. After a period of intense conflict or emotional abuse, the manipulator may shift to love bombing, showering their partner with affection to keep them emotionally invested.
- Blaming the Victim: Manipulators in toxic relationships often refuse to take

responsibility for their actions, instead blaming their partner for any issues in the relationship. This might involve statements like, "You're too sensitive," or "If you weren't so difficult, we wouldn't have these problems."

- Isolation: Manipulators frequently isolate their partners from friends, family, and social networks to make them more dependent. They may discourage social interactions, criticize the victim's loved ones, or create drama that causes the victim to cut ties with others.

Responding to Toxic Relationships

Once you recognize that you are in a toxic relationship, it's important to take steps to protect yourself and, if necessary, remove yourself from the situation. Leaving a toxic relationship can be difficult, especially if you are emotionally or financially dependent on the manipulator.

However, with the right support and strategies, it is possible to regain control of your life.

Steps to Respond to Toxic Dynamics:

1. Acknowledge the Problem: The first step in responding to a toxic relationship is acknowledging that the dynamics are unhealthy. This can be difficult, especially if the manipulator has been gaslighting or blaming you for the problems in the relationship.

2. Set Boundaries: Establishing clear boundaries is essential in toxic relationships. These boundaries should protect your emotional and physical well-being and prevent the manipulator from exerting further control. However, be prepared for pushback, as manipulators often resist changes that threaten their power.

3. Seek Support: Reach out to friends, family, or a therapist for support. Having a support network can help you gain perspective, build

your confidence, and make it easier to leave the toxic relationship.

4. Consider Ending the Relationship: In some cases, the only way to protect yourself from further harm is to leave the relationship. This can be a difficult and emotional process, but it is often the healthiest option in the long term.

5. Focus on Healing: After leaving a toxic relationship, it's important to focus on healing and rebuilding your sense of self-worth. This may involve therapy, self-care practices, or reconnecting with friends and family who support your well-being.

Toxic manipulation in relationships can take a serious toll on your emotional and psychological health. By understanding emotional manipulation, gaslighting, and power imbalances, you can better protect yourself from harmful dynamics and take steps to cultivate healthier, more equitable relationships.

Chapter 5: Manipulation in the Workplace

The workplace is rife with opportunities for manipulation, from co-workers to managers. Office politics, competition, and ambition often lead to subtle or overt manipulation tactics. This chapter will discuss how to spot and counter manipulation in professional settings, including dealing with passive-aggressive behaviors, credit-stealing, and office power plays.

The workplace is a microcosm of society, filled with various personalities, dynamics, and goals. Whether in a corporate office, retail environment, or any other professional setting, manipulation can often go unnoticed because of its subtle, indirect nature. In many workplaces, manipulation is intertwined with office politics, passive-aggressive behaviors, and hidden agendas that contribute to toxic environments. Understanding these tactics is essential for protecting yourself, managing your career effectively, and ensuring your well-being in the workplace.

In this chapter, we will explore the intricacies of manipulation in the workplace, specifically focusing on office politics, passive-aggressive behaviors, and hidden agendas. We'll also examine strategies for self-protection and negotiation to equip you with the tools needed to navigate these challenges.

Office Politics and Manipulation

Office politics is an unavoidable aspect of any workplace. It refers to the informal and sometimes manipulative strategies individuals use to gain power, influence decisions, or enhance their career prospects. While office politics isn't inherently negative, it often becomes manipulative when people use covert tactics to undermine others or advance their own goals at the expense of their colleagues.

What Are Office Politics?

Office politics encompasses the actions and behaviors that individuals engage in to influence power dynamics, build alliances, and achieve personal or professional goals within an organization. It often involves subtle and covert interactions, where individuals use relationships, information, and authority to maneuver for personal gain.

In environments where office politics thrive, decisions may not always be based on merit, and success often depends on who knows whom, rather than who is the most qualified or deserving. This creates an environment ripe for manipulation, as those skilled in navigating political dynamics often excel at the expense of others who may be more focused on their work than their workplace image.

Common Tactics in Office Politics:

- Forming Alliances and Cliques: One of the most common tactics in office politics is forming alliances with colleagues, especially those in positions of power. These alliances often serve to advance shared interests and provide mutual support in navigating workplace dynamics. However, cliques can also become exclusionary, isolating those who aren't part of the group and making it difficult for outsiders to advance.

- Undermining Others: Manipulators often engage in subtle undermining to weaken a colleague's credibility or performance. This might involve spreading rumors, subtly criticizing others in front of supervisors, or pointing out minor mistakes to make someone seem incompetent.

- Taking Credit for Others' Work: One of the most frustrating aspects of office politics is when someone takes credit for work they didn't do. This can be especially damaging in collaborative environments, where individual contributions can be easily overshadowed.

- Backstabbing: Manipulators who engage in backstabbing use two-faced tactics, where they appear supportive to someone's face while secretly working against them behind the scenes. This could involve sabotaging projects, spreading misinformation, or creating division within teams.

The Motivations Behind Office Politics

The motivations behind office politics can range from ambition to insecurity. People who engage in manipulative office politics may feel threatened by others, fear losing power, or have a strong desire for career advancement. In some cases, individuals may use office politics to protect their job security or gain influence over organizational decisions.

Key Motivations:

- Career Advancement: Many individuals engage in office politics to gain promotions, salary increases, or more desirable assignments. By leveraging relationships and manipulating situations, they may seek to position themselves for career success at the expense of their colleagues.

- Power and Control: Power dynamics are a significant motivator in office politics. Those who are motivated by a desire for control may engage in manipulation to maintain their influence within the organization or to position themselves as indispensable.

- Job Security: In uncertain job markets or competitive industries, some individuals may use office politics as a means of protecting their job security. By aligning themselves with powerful individuals or undermining potential rivals, they may feel more secure in their position.

The Impact of Manipulation in Office Politics

Office politics can have far-reaching effects on both individuals and the organization as a whole. Manipulation often creates an environment of distrust, competition, and division, undermining teamwork and collaboration. When manipulation becomes entrenched in office politics, it can also lead to a toxic work culture where merit and performance are overshadowed by personal alliances and covert tactics.

Negative Effects of Manipulative Office Politics:

- Decreased Morale: Employees who feel they are being manipulated or undermined by office politics often experience decreased morale. This can lead to disengagement, dissatisfaction with their job, and even burnout.

- Reduced Collaboration: Manipulation in office politics can hinder collaboration, as employees may become more focused on protecting themselves or advancing their own interests rather than working together toward common goals.

- Increased Turnover: A manipulative work environment can drive talented employees to leave the organization in search of a healthier workplace. High turnover can be costly for the organization, both in terms of lost talent and the time required to recruit and train new employees.

- Damaged Reputations: For those who become the target of office politics, their professional reputation may be unfairly damaged. This can make it difficult for them to advance in their careers, both within the organization and in future opportunities.

Passive-Aggressive Behaviors and Hidden Agendas

Passive-aggressive behavior is a common form of manipulation in the workplace. Unlike direct aggression, which is overt and confrontational, passive-aggressive behaviors are subtle and indirect. They are often characterized by resentment or hostility that is expressed in a covert manner, making it difficult for the target to address the issue directly.

What is Passive-Aggressive Behavior?

Passive-aggressive behavior is a pattern of expressing negative feelings or resistance through indirect actions rather than open communication. In the workplace, passive-aggressive behavior can manifest in various ways, from procrastination to backhanded compliments, or even sabotage of a colleague's efforts. This type of behavior is particularly damaging because it is often difficult to confront, leaving the target feeling confused, frustrated, and powerless.

Common Passive-Aggressive Behaviors in the Workplace:

- Procrastination and Delaying Tactics: One of the most common forms of passive-aggressive behavior is intentionally delaying tasks or deadlines. This might be done to frustrate a colleague, sabotage a project, or avoid responsibility.

- Sarcasm and Backhanded Compliments: Passive-aggressive individuals often use sarcasm or backhanded compliments to express their resentment or frustration. For example, they might say, "Well, aren't you the office superstar?" in a sarcastic tone, implying jealousy or criticism.

- Withholding Information: Another passive-aggressive tactic is deliberately withholding important information that could impact a project's success. This might involve "forgetting" to forward an important email or failing to share key updates in a meeting.

- Playing the Victim: Some passive-aggressive individuals use victimhood as a way to avoid taking responsibility for their actions. They may exaggerate the difficulties they're facing or claim that others are treating them unfairly to deflect attention from their own behavior.

- Sabotage and Undermining Efforts: In more extreme cases, passive-aggressive individuals may engage in subtle sabotage, such as intentionally making mistakes or causing disruptions that negatively impact a colleague's performance.

Hidden Agendas in the Workplace

A hidden agenda occurs when an individual pursues personal goals or objectives that are not aligned with the stated goals of the team or organization. These agendas are often concealed, making it difficult for others to understand the true motivations behind certain actions or decisions. Hidden agendas can be especially damaging in collaborative environments, as they create mistrust and undermine team cohesion.

Examples of Hidden Agendas:

- Personal Ambition: Employees with hidden agendas may be more focused on their own career advancement than on the success of the team or organization. They may manipulate situations to position themselves for promotions, salary increases, or special projects, even if it means sabotaging others.
- Undermining Competitors: Some individuals may have a hidden agenda to undermine colleagues they perceive as rivals. This might

involve spreading rumors, criticizing their work behind their back, or positioning themselves as the "go-to" person for management.

- Influence and Control: In some cases, individuals with hidden agendas may seek to gain influence or control within the organization. This could involve manipulating team dynamics, fostering divisions, or aligning themselves with key decision-makers to enhance their power.

The Impact of Passive-Aggressive Behavior and Hidden Agendas

Passive-aggressive behaviors and hidden agendas can have a significant impact on workplace dynamics. These behaviors create confusion and frustration, making it difficult for teams to work together effectively. In addition, they can lead to a toxic work environment where employees feel like they're constantly walking on eggshells, unsure of who they can trust.

Negative Effects of Passive-Aggressive Behavior and Hidden Agendas:

- Erosion of Trust: Passive-aggressive behaviors and hidden agendas undermine trust between colleagues. When employees feel that others are not being honest or are working against the team's goals, collaboration breaks down, and relationships become strained.

- Increased Tension and Frustration: Dealing with passive-aggressive individuals or those with hidden agendas can be incredibly frustrating. The indirect nature of their behavior makes it difficult to address issues directly, leading to unresolved conflicts and tension.

- Reduced Productivity: When passive-aggressive behaviors and hidden agendas are present, productivity often suffers. Teams may struggle to meet deadlines or complete projects efficiently because of delays, sabotage, or a lack of open communication.

- Toxic Work Environment: Over time, passive-aggressive behaviors and hidden agendas can contribute to a toxic work environment. Employees may become disengaged, demoralized, or even fearful of speaking up, further perpetuating a cycle of negativity and manipulation.

Strategies for Self-Protection and Negotiation

Navigating a workplace where manipulation, passive-aggressive behavior, and hidden agendas are present requires self-awareness, assertiveness, and strategic thinking. To protect yourself and manage these dynamics effectively, it's important to develop communication skills, set boundaries, and learn how to negotiate in a way that protects your interests without escalating conflict.

Self-Protection in the Workplace

Protecting yourself from manipulation in the workplace begins with recognizing the signs of manipulation and taking proactive steps to assert your boundaries. By staying vigilant and maintaining a strong sense of self, you can avoid becoming a target of office politics or passive-aggressive behavior.

Tips for Self-Protection:

1. Recognize the Manipulation Tactics: The first step in protecting yourself is being able to identify when manipulation is occurring. Whether it's through subtle undermining, withholding information, or passive-aggressive behavior, being able to recognize these tactics will help you respond effectively.

2. Set Clear Boundaries: Establishing clear boundaries with colleagues is essential in preventing manipulation. For example, if someone is constantly pushing you to take on extra work or share confidential information, it's important to assert your limits and protect your time and resources.

3. Stay Focused on Your Work: One of the best ways to protect yourself from office politics is to remain focused on your work and performance. While it's important to be aware of the political dynamics in your workplace, getting too caught up in them can be distracting and detrimental to your career.

4. Document Key Interactions: When dealing with passive-aggressive individuals or those with hidden agendas, it can be helpful to document key conversations, emails, or meetings. Keeping a record of interactions can protect you in case of disputes or if someone attempts to misrepresent what was said or agreed upon.

5. Build a Support Network: Having allies in the workplace can provide a buffer against manipulation. Whether it's trusted colleagues, mentors, or supervisors, building a support network can help you navigate difficult situations and protect your professional reputation.

Assertive Communication

Assertive communication is a powerful tool for navigating manipulation and office politics. It involves expressing your needs, opinions, and boundaries clearly and confidently without being aggressive. By communicating assertively, you can address issues directly while maintaining professionalism and respect.

Key Principles of Assertive Communication:

1. Be Clear and Direct: When communicating with colleagues, supervisors, or teams, it's important to be clear and direct about your needs, expectations, and boundaries. Avoid being vague or passive, as this can leave room for manipulation.

2. Use "I" Statements: When addressing a conflict or issue, use "I" statements to express your feelings without blaming others. For example, say, "I feel frustrated when deadlines are missed," rather than, "You always miss deadlines."

3. Stay Calm and Composed: Assertive communication is most effective when delivered calmly and confidently. Avoid raising your voice or becoming defensive, as this can escalate the situation or be perceived as aggressive.

4. Listen Actively: Being assertive also means being a good listener. When addressing conflicts or negotiating, take the time to listen to the other person's perspective, even if you don't agree with it. This shows respect and can help de-escalate tension.

Negotiation Strategies

Negotiation is a critical skill in the workplace, whether you're advocating for a promotion, managing conflict, or navigating office politics. Effective negotiation requires preparation, clear communication, and the ability to find mutually beneficial solutions.

Tips for Effective Negotiation:

1. Know Your Worth: Before entering any negotiation, it's important to know your value and what you bring to the table. This is particularly important when negotiating salary, promotions, or job responsibilities.

2. Be Prepared: Successful negotiation requires thorough preparation. Know what you want, what you're willing to compromise on, and what your bottom line is before entering the conversation.

3. Focus on Solutions, Not Problems: When negotiating, focus on finding solutions that benefit both parties rather than dwelling on the problem. For example, if you're negotiating a raise, frame the conversation around the value you bring to the company and how a raise would benefit both you and the organization.

4. Don't Be Afraid to Walk Away: In some cases, the best negotiation tactic is being willing to walk away. If the other party is unwilling to compromise or meet your needs,

it's important to know when to step back and explore other options.

Conclusion

Manipulation in the workplace can take many forms, from subtle office politics to more overt passive-aggressive behaviors and hidden agendas. These dynamics can create a toxic work environment, eroding trust, collaboration, and productivity. However, by recognizing manipulation tactics, setting clear boundaries, and using assertive communication and negotiation strategies, you can protect yourself and navigate the complexities of the modern workplace with confidence. Ultimately, building healthy relationships and maintaining your professional integrity will help you succeed even in the most challenging environments.

Chapter 6: Manipulation in Advertising and Marketing

Advertising and marketing are pervasive in modern life. From the moment we wake up to the moment we go to sleep, we are bombarded with messages designed to influence our thoughts, emotions, and decisions. While advertising is essential for businesses to promote their products and services, the tactics used can sometimes blur the line between ethical persuasion and manipulative strategies. Companies often employ psychological tricks, manipulate our sense of urgency or scarcity, and tap into our emotional vulnerabilities to steer our choices in ways that may not always be in our best interest.

This chapter will explore how manipulation works in advertising and marketing by delving into psychological tricks, the creation of false scarcity and urgency, and methods to maintain control over your consumer decisions. Understanding these tactics will empower you to make more informed and conscious choices in a marketplace where manipulation often goes unnoticed.

Psychological Tricks in Advertising

Advertising taps into various psychological principles to influence consumers' decisions. By understanding how the human brain processes information, advertisers can craft messages that resonate on a deeper emotional level, persuading people to buy products or services they might not have otherwise considered. While not all advertising is inherently manipulative, some techniques are designed to exploit cognitive biases, emotional responses, and subconscious motivations.

1. The Mere Exposure Effect

The mere exposure effect is a psychological phenomenon where people tend to develop a preference for things simply because they are familiar with them. This principle plays a crucial role in advertising strategies that involve repetitive exposure to brands or products. The more often you see an ad, hear a brand's jingle, or encounter a product's logo, the more likely you are to develop a positive attitude toward that brand or product.

How It's Used:

- Repetition in Ads: Advertisers often bombard consumers with the same messages over and over again, reinforcing the brand's presence in the consumer's mind. Think about how often you see certain fast-food chains advertised on television, billboards, and social media. Over time, this repetition builds familiarity, making consumers more likely to choose that brand when making a purchase decision.

- Brand Placement: Companies also use product placements in movies, TV shows, or influencer content to increase familiarity. The subtle inclusion of a product in everyday scenes increases the likelihood that consumers will associate the brand with positive emotions or experiences.

Impact on Consumers: The mere exposure effect can make consumers feel more comfortable with certain brands, even if they haven't consciously evaluated the quality or value of the product. This can lead to habitual purchasing decisions based on familiarity rather than an objective assessment of the product's merits.

2. Social Proof

Social proof is the psychological principle that people tend to follow the actions or behaviors of others, especially when they are uncertain about what to do. In advertising, social proof is used to persuade consumers that a product or service is desirable because others have already deemed it worthy.

How It's Used:

- Testimonials and Reviews: One of the most common uses of social proof in advertising is customer testimonials or product reviews. When potential customers see positive feedback from others, especially from people they perceive as similar to themselves, they are more likely to trust the product and make a purchase.

- Influencer Marketing: Brands often partner with influencers—celebrities, social media personalities, or respected figures in a particular niche—to promote products. The idea is that if someone admired or trusted by a large following uses and endorses a product, consumers will be more likely to buy it as well.

- "Best-Seller" Labels: Retailers frequently highlight best-selling items, implying that these products are popular for a reason. This can lead consumers to choose these items over others, believing that if so many people are buying them, they must be the best choice.

Impact on Consumers: Social proof can create a herd mentality, where consumers feel pressured to conform to popular opinion rather than make decisions based on their own preferences or research. This can lead to impulse purchases, particularly in online shopping environments where positive reviews are prominently displayed.

3. Emotional Appeals

Emotions play a significant role in decision-making, and advertisers know this well. Emotional appeals are designed to elicit specific feelings—whether it's happiness, nostalgia, fear, or desire—that drive consumers to take action.

How It's Used:

- Fear and Safety: Some advertisements use fear to manipulate consumers into buying products. For example, insurance companies might create ads that highlight the dangers of not being adequately insured, tapping into consumers' fears of financial ruin or unexpected disasters.

- Happiness and Aspiration: Many ads use images of people enjoying life, feeling fulfilled, or achieving success to create an association between the product and happiness. For example, advertisements for luxury cars often show happy, successful individuals driving through scenic locations, implying that owning the car will lead to a similarly fulfilling lifestyle.

- Nostalgia: Brands sometimes evoke nostalgia to appeal to consumers' emotional connection to the past. This can be especially effective with older consumers, who may associate a brand with happy memories from their childhood or younger years.

Impact on Consumers: Emotional appeals can bypass rational thinking, making consumers more likely to make decisions based on how they feel in the moment rather than what makes the most sense for their needs. This can lead to purchases driven by impulsive emotional responses rather than careful consideration of the product's value.

4. The Scarcity Principle

The scarcity principle is the idea that people value things more when they perceive them to be scarce or limited. This taps into the fear of missing out (FOMO), a powerful emotional driver in consumer behavior.

How It's Used:

- Limited-Time Offers: Advertisements often create a sense of urgency by promoting "limited-time offers" or "flash sales." The implication is that if you don't act quickly, you'll miss out on a great deal.
- Exclusive Products: Some brands position their products as exclusive or limited-edition, making them seem more desirable because not everyone can have them. This can create

a sense of status or uniqueness for those who manage to obtain the product.

Impact on Consumers: The scarcity principle can make consumers feel pressured to make a quick decision without taking the time to evaluate whether they really need the product. This can lead to impulse buying, especially in online shopping, where limited-time deals and flash sales are common.

Creating False Scarcity and Urgency

Scarcity and urgency are powerful psychological triggers that compel consumers to act quickly, often without fully thinking through their decisions. While legitimate scarcity—such as a genuinely limited supply of a product—can drive demand, advertisers frequently create false scarcity to manipulate consumers into making purchases they might not have otherwise considered.

1. False Scarcity in Advertising

False scarcity occurs when advertisers or companies artificially limit the availability of a product or create the illusion that demand is higher than it actually is. This tactic plays on consumers' fear of missing out, pushing them to act immediately rather than risk losing the opportunity.

Examples of False Scarcity:

- "Only a Few Left!" Notifications: E-commerce websites often display messages like "Only 3 left in stock!" or "Limited quantities available!" even when there is no actual shortage of the product. This creates a sense of urgency, making consumers feel that if they don't buy now, the item will soon be gone.
- Artificially Limited Supply: Some companies manufacture a limited supply of a product, not because of actual production constraints, but to create the illusion of exclusivity. This is common with luxury goods or high-demand

items like sneakers, where the perception of scarcity drives up desire and price.

- Countdown Timers: Online stores often use countdown timers for sales or discounts, giving the impression that the deal will expire soon. In reality, these timers may reset once the countdown ends, or the sale may be extended indefinitely.

Impact on Consumers: False scarcity manipulates consumers into making quick, emotionally driven decisions out of fear that the opportunity will disappear. This can lead to impulse buying and buyer's remorse, as consumers realize later that they were pressured into a purchase they didn't really want or need.

2. Creating a Sense of Urgency

Creating a sense of urgency is another common tactic used in advertising to push consumers into immediate action. Urgency can be real, such as during an end-of-season sale, but it is often artificially created through time-limited promotions, exclusive offers, and countdown clocks.

Examples of Urgency Tactics:

- "Today Only" Sales: Retailers frequently use one-day sales or flash sales to encourage consumers to buy immediately. The implication is that the offer won't be available tomorrow, prompting people to act without taking the time to compare prices or consider alternatives.

- Pre-Order Bonuses: Some companies offer bonuses or discounts for customers who pre-order a product before its official release. This creates a sense of urgency to place an order before the product is even available, tapping into the excitement of being among the first to own it.

- Urgent Messaging in Ads: Words like "Hurry," "Don't Miss Out," or "Act Now" are commonly used in advertisements to create a sense of urgency. These messages are designed to trigger a fear response, making consumers feel that they need to act quickly to avoid missing out.

Impact on Consumers: Urgency tactics can lead consumers to make rushed decisions without fully evaluating whether they need or want the product. In many cases, consumers may regret their purchases once the perceived urgency has passed and they've had more time to reflect.

How to Maintain Control Over Consumer Decisions

In a marketplace filled with manipulative tactics, it can be challenging to maintain control over your consumer decisions. However, by understanding the psychological tricks that advertisers use and implementing strategies to resist them, you can become a more empowered and informed consumer. Here are several key strategies for maintaining control over your purchasing decisions:

1. Recognize Manipulative Tactics

The first step in maintaining control over your consumer decisions is recognizing when advertisers are using manipulative tactics. By becoming aware of psychological tricks such as social proof, scarcity, and emotional appeals, you can critically evaluate advertisements and avoid being swayed by manipulative messaging.

How to Spot Manipulative Tactics:

- Be Aware of Repetition: If you notice that you're seeing the same ad or brand message repeatedly, ask yourself whether your familiarity with the brand is influencing your perception of its quality or value.

- Question Social Proof: Before making a purchase based on positive reviews or testimonials, consider whether the reviews are genuine or if influencers have been paid to promote the product. Look for reviews from multiple sources and verify their authenticity.

- Watch for False Scarcity and Urgency: Be skeptical of countdown timers, limited-time offers, or notifications that claim an item is almost sold out. Check other websites or retailers to see if the product is truly in short supply or if the sale is genuinely time-limited.

2. Take Your Time to Make Decisions

One of the most effective ways to avoid falling prey to manipulative advertising is to take your time before making a purchase decision. Advertisers often rely on creating a sense of urgency to push consumers into acting quickly, but by slowing down and thinking critically, you can regain control over your choices.

Strategies for Slowing Down:

- Use a 24-Hour Rule: Before making any non-essential purchase, give yourself at least 24 hours to think it over. This cooling-off period allows you to evaluate whether you really need the product or if you're being swayed by emotional or manipulative tactics.

- Avoid Impulse Buys: When shopping online, avoid adding items to your cart impulsively. Instead, create a wishlist or bookmark the product and revisit it later. This gives you time to consider whether the purchase is necessary or if you're being influenced by advertising.

- Compare Prices: Take the time to compare prices across different retailers before making a purchase. Often, limited-time offers or flash sales aren't as exclusive as they seem, and you may be able to find the same product at a lower price elsewhere.

3. Focus on Your Needs, Not Wants

Advertisers are skilled at creating desires for products we don't necessarily need. To maintain control over your decisions, it's important to distinguish between your needs and wants. By focusing on what you truly need, you can avoid being swayed by advertising that appeals to your emotional desires.

How to Prioritize Needs:

- Make a Shopping List: Before making any purchases, create a list of items you need. This helps you stay focused and prevents you from being tempted by products that aren't on your list.
- Ask Yourself Key Questions: Before buying something, ask yourself, "Do I really need this?" and "Will this product improve my life in a meaningful way?" These questions help you think critically about your purchases and avoid buying things based on emotional impulses.
- Set a Budget: Establish a budget for non-essential purchases each month and stick to it. This forces you to prioritize your spending and avoid unnecessary splurges driven by advertising.

4. Practice Mindful Consumerism

Mindful consumerism involves being intentional and thoughtful about your purchasing decisions. It's about considering the impact of your choices, not only on your own life but also on the environment, society, and economy. By practicing mindful consumerism, you can resist manipulative tactics and make choices that align with your values.

How to Be a Mindful Consumer:

- Research Before Buying: Before making a purchase, take the time to research the company and its products. Consider factors such as sustainability, ethical sourcing, and corporate social responsibility. This ensures that your purchases align with your values and aren't just driven by advertising.
- Support Local and Small Businesses: Instead of buying from large corporations that use manipulative advertising tactics, consider supporting local or small businesses that

prioritize quality, transparency, and ethical practices.

- Avoid Consumerism for the Sake of It: Advertisers often create a sense of "keeping up with the Joneses" by making consumers feel like they need the latest products to fit in or be successful. By rejecting this mindset and focusing on what truly matters to you, you can avoid being manipulated into unnecessary purchases.

5. Use Technology to Your Advantage

In the digital age, technology can both contribute to and help combat advertising manipulation. While online platforms often track consumer behavior and target individuals with personalized ads, there are also tools available that can help you regain control over your online shopping experience.

Helpful Tools and Strategies:

- Ad Blockers: Use ad-blocking software or browser extensions to reduce the number of advertisements you see online. This can help limit the influence of targeted ads and prevent you from being bombarded by manipulative messages.

- Price-Tracking Tools: There are several apps and websites that allow you to track the prices of products over time, helping you identify whether a sale is truly a good deal or if the price has been artificially inflated before being "discounted."

- Unsubscribe from Marketing Emails: If you find yourself frequently tempted by marketing emails, consider unsubscribing from mailing lists that promote frequent sales or limited-time offers. This reduces the number of ads you're exposed to and helps you focus on your own needs rather than external pressures.

Conclusion

Manipulation in advertising and marketing is pervasive, but by understanding the psychological tricks, false scarcity, and urgency tactics that companies use, you can take control of your consumer decisions. By recognizing these manipulative techniques, slowing down your decision-making process, and practicing mindful consumerism, you can make more informed and empowered choices that align with your values and needs, rather than being swayed by emotional appeals or fear of missing out. The more conscious you become of these tactics, the better equipped you will be to navigate the marketplace with confidence and intention.

Part 3: Protecting Yourself from Manipulation

Chapter 7: Recognizing Manipulation

Manipulation is a subtle, yet powerful form of control that can have a deep impact on our personal and professional lives. It often disguises itself under the appearance of good intentions, making it difficult to identify. Manipulative individuals use tactics like coercion, deceit, and undue influence to control the behaviors, emotions, and decisions of others. Recognizing manipulation is the first step toward protecting yourself from its harmful effects. In this chapter, we will explore the red flags of manipulation, how to spot coercion, deceit, and undue influence, and how to trust your instincts while using logic to counter manipulation.

Red Flags of Manipulation

Manipulation can be so subtle that it often goes unnoticed, especially in relationships where trust and emotional connection are involved. However, there are certain red flags that can help you identify when someone is trying to manipulate you. These red flags often show up in the form of emotional manipulation, behavioral control, or psychological pressure. Being able to recognize these signs is crucial to regaining control over your own decisions and protecting your autonomy.

1. Emotional Blackmail

Emotional blackmail is one of the most common forms of manipulation. It involves using fear, guilt, or obligation to force someone to comply with the manipulator's wishes. The manipulator may position themselves as a victim, leveraging your emotions to make you feel responsible for their well-being or happiness.

Signs of Emotional Blackmail:

- **Guilt-Tripping:** Manipulators often make you feel guilty for not doing something they want. They may remind you of past favors or sacrifices, implying that you owe them something in return.

- Example: "After everything I've done for you, you can't even help me with this one thing?"

- Fear-Based Manipulation: A manipulator may use fear to pressure you into compliance, threatening negative consequences if you don't act according to their demands.

  - Example: "If you don't help me, I don't know what I'll do. You'll be responsible if something bad happens."

- Silent Treatment: The silent treatment is a passive-aggressive tactic where the manipulator withdraws communication and affection, leaving you feeling isolated until you give in to their demands.

2. Gaslighting

Gaslighting is a particularly insidious form of manipulation where the manipulator distorts reality, making the victim question their own perceptions, memories, and even sanity. The goal of gaslighting is to create doubt and confusion, making the victim more dependent on the manipulator for a sense of reality.

Signs of Gaslighting:

- Denying Reality: The manipulator blatantly denies things that have happened, even when there is clear evidence. They may say things like, "That never happened," or "You're imagining things."
- Minimizing Your Feelings: Gaslighters often belittle your feelings, telling you that you're overreacting or being too sensitive.
  - Example: "You're just being dramatic. It's not as bad as you're making it out to be."
- Rewriting the Narrative: The manipulator may twist events to make it seem like you're at fault or that you misunderstood the situation.
  - Example: "You're remembering it wrong. That's not what I said."

Gaslighting can be especially harmful because it erodes your sense of trust in yourself, making you question your own reality and leading to increased dependence on the manipulator.

3. Love Bombing and Devaluation

Love bombing is a tactic where a manipulator overwhelms you with affection, attention, and praise in the early stages of a relationship. This excessive affection can create a strong emotional bond and a sense of dependency. However, once the manipulator has you under their control, they often switch to devaluation, where they criticize, belittle, or withdraw affection, leaving you feeling confused and insecure.

Signs of Love Bombing:

- **Excessive Praise and Attention:** The manipulator showers you with compliments, gifts, and attention, often moving the relationship forward too quickly.

- Example: "You're the most amazing person I've ever met. I can't believe how lucky I am to have found you."

- Pushing for Commitment: Love bombers may push for a commitment early on, pressuring you to move in together or make big life decisions before you're ready.

  - Example: "We should move in together. Why wait when we both know this is special?"

Signs of Devaluation:

- Sudden Withdrawal of Affection: Once the manipulator feels secure in the relationship, they may abruptly withdraw affection or attention, leaving you feeling confused and anxious.

  - Example: "I don't know why you're so needy all of a sudden. I need space."

- Criticism and Belittling: After the initial love bombing phase, the manipulator may begin to criticize you or make you feel unworthy.

- Example: "You're not as smart as I thought you were. I don't know why I even bother."

- The cycle of love bombing and devaluation can be deeply destabilizing, as the highs of the love-bombing phase make the lows of the devaluation phase even more painful.

4. Overstepping Boundaries

Manipulators often push or ignore personal boundaries to gain control. They may act in ways that make you uncomfortable, but they will often minimize your concerns or make you feel unreasonable for trying to enforce boundaries.

Signs of Overstepping Boundaries:

- Ignoring Personal Space or Privacy: The manipulator may invade your personal space or privacy without your consent, such as going through your phone or showing up unannounced.

- Pushing for More Than You're Comfortable With: Manipulators may push for emotional, physical, or financial commitments before you're ready.
  - Example: "Why are you being so difficult? If you really cared about me, you wouldn't have a problem with this."

Boundaries are essential for healthy relationships, and any attempt to overstep or ignore them should be seen as a red flag of manipulation.

Spotting Coercion, Deceit, and Undue Influence

In addition to more overt forms of manipulation, coercion, deceit, and undue influence are often used to subtly steer your decisions or behavior. These tactics are more difficult to spot because they are often disguised as persuasion, concern, or even helpfulness. Understanding how to recognize these forms of manipulation can help you avoid being controlled or coerced into actions that aren't in your best interest.

1. Coercion

Coercion occurs when someone uses threats, pressure, or intimidation to force you to act in a way that benefits them. Unlike persuasion, which is based on mutual understanding and respect, coercion leaves you feeling trapped or powerless.

Signs of Coercion:

- **Implied or Direct Threats:** Coercion often involves threats, either explicit or implied. The manipulator may threaten to end a relationship, withhold something you value, or cause harm if you don't comply.
  - Example: "If you don't do this, I'll make sure you lose your job."
- **Emotional Pressure:** Coercive manipulators may apply emotional pressure by making you feel responsible for their well-being or happiness.
  - Example: "If you leave me, I'll fall apart. You're the only thing keeping me going."

- Creating a No-Win Situation: Coercion often involves creating a false choice where all options lead to the same outcome, making you feel as though you have no real say in the matter.
  - Example: "Either you do this, or you can forget about our future together."

Coercion can lead to significant emotional distress, as the manipulator's demands often escalate over time, leaving you feeling increasingly controlled.

2. Deceit

Deceit is another key element of manipulation, involving the intentional distortion or concealment of facts to influence your decisions. A deceitful manipulator will mislead you by providing false information, omitting important details, or spinning the truth to serve their own interests.

Signs of Deceit:

- Lying or Omitting Information: Manipulators often lie or leave out critical information to deceive you. They may downplay the negative aspects of a situation or exaggerate the benefits to get you on board.
  - Example: "I didn't think it was necessary to tell you about that part. It's not a big deal."
- Contradicting Themselves: Manipulators often get caught in their own lies. If someone frequently changes their story or contradicts themselves, it's a sign that they are being deceitful.
  - Example: "Wait, I thought you said the meeting was canceled?" "Oh, no, I meant it was moved."
- Fake Sincerity: Some manipulators use false sincerity to gain your trust, pretending to be honest and transparent while secretly deceiving you.
  - Example: "I'm telling you this because I care about you. You can trust me."

- Deceit can be especially harmful in relationships, as it erodes trust and leaves you questioning what is real and what is false.

3. Undue Influence

Undue influence occurs when someone uses their position of power, authority, or trust to manipulate your decisions. Unlike overt coercion, undue influence is often more subtle, taking advantage of your trust or dependence on the manipulator.

Signs of Undue Influence:

- Manipulating a Position of Authority: If someone holds a position of power—whether as a boss, mentor, or even a trusted friend—they may use that authority to influence your decisions. They might frame their suggestions as "for your own good" or imply that you owe them compliance due to their superior position.

- Example: "I've been in this business for years. Trust me, this is what you need to do."
- Leveraging Emotional Dependency: Manipulators who know you rely on them emotionally may use that dependence to sway your decisions.
  - Example: "You know I'm the only one who really understands you. Without me, you'd be lost."
- Creating a False Sense of Obligation: Manipulators often make you feel obligated to follow their lead because they've done something for you in the past or have helped you in some way.
  - Example: "After everything I've done for you, you really think you can just ignore my advice?"

Undue influence is particularly dangerous because it often occurs in relationships where trust, power dynamics, or dependency are already present, making it difficult to recognize as manipulation.

Trusting Your Instincts and Using Logic

One of the most effective ways to recognize and resist manipulation is to trust your instincts and use logic to evaluate the situation. Manipulators often try to distort reality, confuse you, or make you doubt your own judgment. By learning to trust your gut feelings and applying rational thinking, you can protect yourself from being manipulated.

1. Trusting Your Instincts

Your instincts, often referred to as your "gut feelings," can be an important tool in recognizing manipulation. If something feels off or makes you uncomfortable, it's essential to pay attention to those feelings. While it's possible that you're misinterpreting a situation, your instincts are often your mind's way of signaling that something is wrong.

Signs That Your Instincts Are Telling You
Something:

- Unexplained Anxiety: If you feel anxious or uneasy around someone but can't pinpoint why, it could be a sign that your instincts are picking up on manipulative behavior.

- A Sense of Confusion: Manipulation often leaves you feeling confused, as the manipulator may distort reality or give conflicting messages. If you frequently feel unsure of what's happening in a relationship or situation, it's worth investigating whether manipulation is at play.

- Feeling Drained: Manipulative relationships can be emotionally exhausting. If you find yourself feeling drained, resentful, or frustrated after interacting with someone, it's important to examine whether manipulation is the cause.

While it's essential to listen to your instincts, it's equally important to use logic to analyze the situation and confirm whether manipulation is actually occurring.

2. Using Logic to Counter Manipulation

Manipulators rely on emotional responses to control their targets. By engaging your logical thinking, you can break free from the emotional manipulation and evaluate the situation more objectively.

Steps for Using Logic:

1. Assess the Facts: Take a step back and assess the situation based on facts, not emotions. What are the concrete details of the situation? Are there inconsistencies in what the manipulator is saying or doing? Has their behavior changed over time?

2. Identify Patterns: Manipulators often use the same tactics repeatedly. Look for patterns of behavior that may indicate manipulation,

such as frequent guilt-tripping, gaslighting, or boundary-pushing.

3. Ask Critical Questions: Challenge the manipulator's narrative by asking yourself critical questions:

    - Does this person's behavior benefit them more than it benefits me?

    - Are they trying to pressure or rush me into a decision?

    - Do they respect my boundaries, or do they continually push against them?

4. Consult a Trusted Friend or Mentor: Sometimes, it's difficult to see manipulation when you're in the middle of it. Talking to a trusted friend, family member, or mentor can provide you with an outside perspective and help you see the situation more clearly.

5. Evaluate the Consequences: Consider the potential consequences of giving in to the manipulator's demands. Are you compromising your values, well-being, or happiness to satisfy someone else's agenda?

3. Balancing Instinct and Logic

While instincts can guide you to recognize manipulation, logic allows you to confirm and counteract it. The key to protecting yourself is balancing these two approaches. Trust your gut when something feels wrong, but always use logical thinking to verify your feelings and decide on the best course of action.

How to Balance Instinct and Logic:

- Pause Before Reacting: If you suspect manipulation, take a moment to pause and reflect before reacting emotionally. Give yourself time to evaluate the situation logically and decide on an appropriate response.
- Practice Self-Awareness: Self-awareness is essential for recognizing when your emotions are being manipulated. By staying attuned to your feelings and reactions, you can better identify when someone is trying to manipulate you.

- Stay Grounded in Reality: Manipulators often try to distort reality or create confusion. Ground yourself in what you know to be true and rely on facts and evidence to guide your decisions.

Conclusion

Recognizing manipulation is a critical step in protecting yourself from its harmful effects. By learning to identify the red flags of manipulation, spotting coercion, deceit, and undue influence, and trusting your instincts while using logic, you can take control of your own decisions and safeguard your emotional and mental well-being. Manipulation thrives in environments where confusion, doubt, and emotional pressure exist, but by staying vigilant and developing critical thinking skills, you can resist these tactics and maintain your autonomy.

Chapter 8: Building Resilience

Once you've identified manipulation, it's essential to build psychological and emotional resilience to counter it effectively. Resilience is the ability to withstand and recover from difficult situations, stress, and manipulation without compromising your emotional or mental well-being. In a world where manipulation is pervasive, building resilience is crucial to protect yourself and maintain control over your thoughts, emotions, and actions.

Resilience isn't just about surviving manipulation but thriving despite it—maintaining your sense of self and using challenges as opportunities for growth. In this chapter, we will explore the importance of self-awareness and emotional intelligence, techniques for managing stress and emotional reactions, and strategies to assert yourself without aggression.

The Importance of Self-Awareness and Emotional Intelligence

Self-awareness and emotional intelligence (EQ) are foundational elements of resilience. They allow you to understand your own emotions and how they influence your behavior, while also helping you navigate interpersonal dynamics with empathy and clarity. When you are self-aware and emotionally intelligent, you can better identify manipulation and regulate your emotional responses to it.

1. What is Self-Awareness?

Self-awareness is the ability to recognize and understand your own emotions, thoughts, and behaviors, and how they affect both you and others. It involves a deep understanding of your strengths, weaknesses, triggers, and motivations, which is critical when facing manipulation. Manipulators often target emotional vulnerabilities, so being aware of these areas can help you avoid falling into their traps.

Components of Self-Awareness:

- Emotional Awareness: Understanding what you're feeling in the moment and being able to name and process those emotions.

- Self-Assessment: Having an honest appraisal of your strengths and weaknesses, knowing what makes you vulnerable to manipulation.

- Self-Confidence: A strong sense of self-worth and capability, which helps you stay grounded when faced with manipulation.

How Self-Awareness Helps with Manipulation:

- Recognizing Emotional Reactions: Self-awareness helps you recognize when you're being emotionally triggered, making it easier to identify when someone is trying to manipulate your feelings.

- Understanding Patterns of Behavior: By being aware of your habitual responses, you can identify patterns that manipulators may exploit, such as tendencies to people-please, avoid conflict, or seek approval.

- Staying Grounded: When you are self-aware, you are less likely to be swayed by external pressures or manipulative tactics, as you have a clear understanding of your own values, goals, and boundaries.

2. Emotional Intelligence (EQ)

Emotional intelligence is the ability to recognize, understand, and manage your own emotions, as well as to understand and influence the emotions of others. It's a critical skill for building resilience because it allows you to navigate difficult interpersonal situations with empathy and clarity, making it harder for others to manipulate or overwhelm you emotionally.

The Four Components of Emotional Intelligence:

1. Self-Awareness: As mentioned earlier, this is the foundation of emotional intelligence, involving an understanding of your emotions and how they influence your behavior.

2. Self-Management: The ability to regulate your emotions, particularly in stressful or challenging situations, without acting impulsively or destructively.

3. Social Awareness: The ability to understand the emotions of others and empathize with them. This helps you read social cues and recognize when someone is attempting to manipulate or deceive you.

4. Relationship Management: The ability to influence and manage relationships effectively, including resolving conflicts and maintaining healthy boundaries.

How Emotional Intelligence Protects You from Manipulation:

- Emotional Regulation: High emotional intelligence helps you regulate your emotional responses, ensuring that you don't react impulsively to manipulative triggers such as guilt, anger, or fear.

- Empathy and Social Awareness: Understanding other people's emotions allows you to detect manipulative intentions or hidden agendas in conversations or interactions.

- Effective Communication: Emotional intelligence helps you communicate your feelings and boundaries assertively without resorting to aggression, which can diffuse manipulative tactics.

3. How to Cultivate Self-Awareness and Emotional Intelligence

Building self-awareness and emotional intelligence requires intentional effort and reflection. By regularly checking in with yourself and practicing empathy toward others, you can enhance these skills over time.

Ways to Cultivate Self-Awareness:

- Reflect on Your Emotional Triggers: Identify situations or behaviors that trigger strong emotional reactions in you. Ask yourself why these triggers affect you and how you can respond more constructively.

- Journaling: Writing down your thoughts and emotions regularly can help you become more attuned to your inner world and recognize patterns in your behavior.

- Mindfulness and Meditation: Practicing mindfulness helps you become more aware of your thoughts and feelings in the present moment, allowing you to observe them without judgment.

- Seek Feedback: Ask trusted friends, colleagues, or mentors for feedback on your behavior. Often, others can provide insight into your strengths and areas for improvement that you may not have noticed.

Ways to Cultivate Emotional Intelligence:

- Practice Empathy: Make a conscious effort to understand how others feel and why they might be acting a certain way. Try to see situations from their perspective, even if you don't agree with them.

- Pause Before Reacting: When faced with a challenging situation, take a moment to pause and reflect on your emotions before responding. This gives you time to regulate your emotions and choose a more thoughtful response.

- Develop Active Listening Skills: Emotional intelligence involves being fully present in conversations, listening actively, and responding with empathy and understanding. This not only helps you build stronger relationships but also helps you detect when someone is being manipulative.

- Work on Emotional Regulation: Learn techniques to manage stress, anger, or anxiety. Emotional regulation is key to maintaining control over your responses, especially when you're facing manipulation or conflict.

Techniques for Managing Stress and Emotional Reactions

Stress and emotional reactions are normal responses to challenging situations, but when unmanaged, they can leave you vulnerable to manipulation. Learning how to manage stress and control your emotional reactions is essential for building resilience and maintaining clarity, even in difficult circumstances. Manipulators often thrive on your emotional reactions, so mastering these techniques will help you maintain control and protect yourself.

1. The Relationship Between Stress and Manipulation

Stress can impair your ability to think clearly and make rational decisions. When you are stressed, your brain goes into "fight-or-flight" mode, which can lead to emotional decision-making rather than logical analysis. Manipulators often exploit stressful situations to steer your decisions in their favor.

How Manipulators Use Stress:

- Creating Pressure: Manipulators may create urgency or stress, pressuring you to make quick decisions without time to think them through.
  - Example: "If you don't agree to this right now, you'll lose the opportunity."
- Triggering Emotional Reactions: Manipulators may provoke emotional responses, such as anger or guilt, to cloud your judgment and make you more likely to comply with their demands.
  - Example: "I can't believe you would do this to me after everything I've done for you!"

Managing stress effectively allows you to maintain control over your reactions and make decisions based on logic and reason rather than emotional pressure.

2. Techniques for Managing Stress

Managing stress involves both immediate strategies for calming yourself in the moment and long-term techniques for reducing overall stress in your life. By incorporating these practices into your routine, you can enhance your resilience and protect yourself from emotional manipulation.

Short-Term Stress Management Techniques:

- Deep Breathing Exercises: Deep breathing helps activate the body's relaxation response, slowing your heart rate and reducing the physical symptoms of stress. Try taking slow, deep breaths for several minutes when you feel overwhelmed.
  - Technique: Inhale deeply through your nose for a count of four, hold your breath for four seconds, and then exhale slowly

through your mouth for a count of four.
Repeat this cycle several times.

- Progressive Muscle Relaxation: This technique involves tensing and then relaxing different muscle groups in your body to release physical tension.

  - Technique: Start with your feet, tense the muscles for five seconds, and then release. Move up through your body—calves, thighs, stomach, chest, arms, and face—repeating the tensing and releasing process.

- Grounding Exercises: Grounding techniques help bring you back to the present moment, reducing anxiety or racing thoughts. One simple method is the 5-4-3-2-1 technique, where you focus on identifying five things you can see, four things you can feel, three things you can hear, two things you can smell, and one thing you can taste.

- Visualization: Visualization techniques can help reduce stress by guiding you through a mental image of a peaceful, relaxing environment. Close your eyes and imagine

yourself in a calming setting, such as a beach
or forest, focusing on the details like sounds,
smells, and sensations.

Long-Term Stress Management Techniques:

- Exercise and Physical Activity: Regular
  physical activity is one of the most effective
  ways to manage stress. Exercise releases
  endorphins, which help improve your mood
  and reduce feelings of anxiety or depression.

- Healthy Eating and Hydration: Maintaining a
  balanced diet and staying hydrated are
  essential for overall well-being. Stress can
  take a toll on your physical health, so fueling
  your body with nutritious foods can help you
  manage stress more effectively.

- Sleep Hygiene: Lack of sleep can exacerbate
  stress and make it more difficult to regulate
  your emotions. Prioritize good sleep hygiene
  by establishing a consistent sleep schedule,
  creating a relaxing bedtime routine, and

minimizing distractions (such as screens) before bed.

- Time Management and Prioritization: Stress often arises when we feel overwhelmed by tasks or responsibilities. Learning to manage your time effectively, break tasks into smaller steps, and prioritize what's most important can reduce feelings of overwhelm.

3. Managing Emotional Reactions

Emotional reactions are natural, but when they go unchecked, they can cloud your judgment and leave you vulnerable to manipulation. Learning how to regulate your emotions, especially in high-stress or high-stakes situations, is key to maintaining control over your actions and decisions.

Techniques for Managing Emotional Reactions:

- Emotional Labeling: One of the most effective ways to regulate emotions is to label them. By identifying and naming what you're feeling—whether it's anger, sadness, frustration, or fear—you reduce the emotional intensity and bring more clarity to the situation.

- Example: Instead of reacting impulsively, say to yourself, "I'm feeling frustrated right now because this person isn't respecting my boundaries."

- Cognitive Reframing: Cognitive reframing involves changing the way you perceive a situation. Rather than seeing yourself as a victim of circumstances, you can reframe the situation as an opportunity for growth or problem-solving.

- Example: If someone is criticizing you, instead of feeling attacked, reframe it as constructive feedback that you can learn from or simply disregard if it's not valid.

- Mindfulness and Staying Present: Mindfulness involves focusing on the present moment without judgment. By staying present, you can prevent your emotions from spiraling out of control and avoid becoming entangled in manipulative tactics.

- Example: If someone is trying to provoke an emotional reaction, take a moment to breathe, observe your feelings without reacting, and choose a calm response.

How to Assert Yourself Without Aggression

One of the most effective tools for protecting yourself from manipulation is assertiveness. Assertiveness allows you to express your needs, desires, and boundaries clearly and confidently without resorting to aggression. It's a communication style that is respectful of both your rights and the rights of others, making it an essential skill in relationships, workplaces, and everyday interactions.

1. The Difference Between Assertiveness, Aggression, and Passivity

Understanding the difference between assertiveness, aggression, and passivity is crucial for finding a balance in your communication style.

- Assertiveness: Assertiveness is the ability to express your needs, feelings, and boundaries in a direct, respectful, and confident manner. It involves standing up for yourself without putting others down or resorting to hostile behavior.
    - Example: "I need more time to complete this project. I will finish it by Friday instead of tomorrow."
- Aggression: Aggression involves expressing your needs in a hostile, confrontational, or disrespectful manner, often at the expense of others. Aggressive behavior can lead to conflict, resentment, and damaged relationships.
    - Example: "You need to finish this now, or there will be serious consequences."

- Passivity: Passivity involves avoiding conflict and not expressing your needs or boundaries, often leading to feelings of resentment or being taken advantage of.
  - Example: "It's fine. I can finish the project today," (even if you don't have the time or resources to do so).

Being assertive without being aggressive allows you to maintain healthy boundaries and communicate effectively, even in challenging situations.

2. How to Be Assertive Without Aggression

Learning how to be assertive without aggression is a key component of building resilience. Assertiveness requires practice and confidence, but it can be developed through intentional effort and clear communication strategies.

Techniques for Assertive Communication:

- Use "I" Statements: "I" statements allow you to express your feelings and needs without sounding accusatory or confrontational. They focus on your experience rather than blaming the other person.

- Example: Instead of saying, "You're always interrupting me," say, "I feel frustrated when I'm interrupted because I can't finish my thoughts."

- Be Direct and Clear: Assertiveness involves being clear and specific about what you need or expect. Avoid beating around the bush or leaving room for interpretation. Be direct, but remain calm and respectful.

  - Example: "I need you to give me at least two days' notice if you need my help with a project. That way, I can manage my workload effectively."

- Maintain Calm Body Language: Non-verbal cues such as body language, eye contact, and tone of voice play a significant role in assertive communication. Keep your posture open and relaxed, maintain eye contact, and speak in a calm, even tone.

- Set Clear Boundaries: Boundaries are essential for maintaining control over your emotional and mental well-being. When you set boundaries assertively, you make it clear what is acceptable and what is not, without being aggressive.

  - Example: "I'm not available to work late on weekends. I can help you with this project during regular working hours."

3. Practicing Assertiveness in Challenging Situations

Being assertive can be particularly challenging when you're dealing with manipulative individuals, high-stakes situations, or power dynamics that make you feel vulnerable. However, practicing assertiveness in these situations is critical for protecting your boundaries and maintaining control.

Steps for Practicing Assertiveness:

1. Prepare Ahead of Time: If you know you're going to be in a challenging situation, prepare ahead of time. Think about what you want to say, how you'll say it, and what boundaries you need to set. Visualize yourself responding calmly and assertively.

2. Stay Calm Under Pressure: When faced with manipulation or aggression, staying calm is key. Take a few deep breaths, ground yourself in the present moment, and remind yourself that you have the right to assert your boundaries.

3. Repeat Your Boundaries If Necessary: Some people may try to test your boundaries or push you to change your mind. In these cases, calmly but firmly repeat your boundary. You don't need to justify or explain your decisions multiple times.

    - Example: "As I mentioned earlier, I'm not available this weekend. We can discuss it on Monday."

4. Know When to Walk Away: If someone
    continues to disrespect your boundaries or
    tries to manipulate you, know that it's okay to
    walk away from the situation. Sometimes,
    removing yourself from a toxic interaction is
    the best form of assertiveness.

Conclusion

Building resilience is an essential part of protecting
yourself from manipulation, managing stress, and
asserting your boundaries in a healthy, confident
manner. By developing self-awareness and
emotional intelligence, learning to manage your
emotional reactions, and practicing assertive
communication, you can maintain control over
your decisions and interactions without resorting to
aggression. These skills will not only help you
defend against manipulation but also empower you
to navigate challenging situations with confidence
and clarity. Resilience is about maintaining your
sense of self in the face of adversity, and by

cultivating these techniques, you can thrive despite
the challenges life throws your way

Chapter 9: Setting Boundaries

Boundaries are essential for protecting yourself from manipulation, maintaining emotional and mental well-being, and fostering healthy relationships. They define what behaviors are acceptable to you and help establish your personal space, both emotionally and physically. In any relationship—whether personal, professional, or social—boundaries set clear expectations, prevent overreach, and ensure mutual respect. Manipulators often target people who struggle to set or maintain boundaries because they see these individuals as easier to control. Understanding the importance of boundaries, learning how to set and enforce them, and handling pushback from boundary violators are critical skills for protecting yourself from manipulation.

In this chapter, we will explore why boundaries are so important, techniques for setting and enforcing them, and how to deal with individuals who resist or violate your limits.

The Importance of Boundaries in Avoiding Manipulation

Boundaries are the invisible lines that separate your needs, desires, values, and personal space from others. They are the foundation of self-respect and mutual respect in relationships, making them a powerful tool for avoiding manipulation. When boundaries are unclear or non-existent, manipulative individuals can easily overstep, exploit vulnerabilities, and exert control over your decisions and emotions.

1. Boundaries Protect Your Autonomy

At their core, boundaries are about autonomy—your right to make decisions about your own life and to have control over your personal space, time, and emotions. When you set boundaries, you define what is and isn't acceptable in your relationships, protecting your autonomy and agency. Without boundaries, you may feel pressured to conform to others' expectations or give in to their demands, often at the expense of your own well-being.

How Manipulators Exploit Weak Boundaries:

- Emotional Manipulation: Manipulators may guilt-trip or pressure you into making decisions that benefit them but harm you, often exploiting your desire to be liked, avoid conflict, or gain approval.

  - Example: "If you really cared about me, you'd help me out with this project, even if it means staying late."

- Boundary Overreach: Manipulators often test the waters by pushing small boundaries to see how much control they can exert. They might ask for a favor that seems innocent at first but escalates into larger demands over time.

  - Example: "Can you take on this one small task for me? I promise it won't take long," followed by repeated requests that drain your time and energy.

When you set firm boundaries, you send a clear message that your needs and values are non-negotiable. This makes it much harder for manipulators to find weak spots to exploit.

2. Boundaries Prevent Emotional Burnout

Without boundaries, you risk becoming emotionally overextended, drained, and overwhelmed by the demands and expectations of others. This is especially true in relationships where one party consistently takes more than they give, leaving the other feeling depleted. Healthy boundaries help you prioritize your emotional well-being, ensuring that you have the time and energy to focus on your own needs without being constantly pulled in different directions.

The Emotional Cost of Poor Boundaries:

- Resentment: When you continually give in to others' demands without setting limits, you may begin to feel resentful, especially if you feel that your needs are being ignored.

- Example: "I always say yes to helping her, but she never seems to appreciate it or offer help in return."
- Stress and Anxiety: Without boundaries, you may find yourself taking on too much responsibility, leading to increased stress and anxiety. Constantly feeling overwhelmed by others' needs can cause emotional burnout.
    - Example: "I don't know how I'll get everything done. Everyone keeps asking me for favors, and I can't say no."

Setting boundaries allows you to protect your emotional energy, ensuring that you have the space to recharge and focus on your own well-being.

3. Boundaries Foster Healthy Relationships

Healthy boundaries are the foundation of mutual respect in relationships. They allow both parties to express their needs, desires, and limitations clearly and respectfully. In contrast, relationships without boundaries often become imbalanced, with one person dominating or controlling the other. Boundaries help create a sense of balance and fairness, where each person's needs are valued and respected.

How Boundaries Improve Relationships:

- Encouraging Open Communication: When boundaries are clearly defined, both parties are more likely to communicate openly and honestly about their needs, reducing misunderstandings and resentment.
  - Example: "I need time to decompress after work before we talk about any major issues. Let's set aside time in the evening to discuss things."
- Promoting Mutual Respect: Boundaries show others how you expect to be treated and signal that you respect yourself. In turn, this encourages others to respect your needs and limits, creating healthier, more balanced relationships.

- Example: "I'm happy to help you, but I need you to ask in advance instead of assuming I'm available."

Techniques for Setting and Enforcing Limits

Setting boundaries may feel uncomfortable, especially if you're not used to advocating for your own needs. However, with practice, setting and enforcing boundaries becomes easier and more natural. The key is to communicate your boundaries clearly and assertively, while also being consistent in enforcing them.

1. Identifying Your Boundaries

The first step in setting boundaries is understanding what they are. Boundaries can be physical, emotional, time-related, or intellectual. They define what is acceptable to you in various aspects of your life and relationships. To identify your boundaries, ask yourself what makes you feel uncomfortable, resentful, or overwhelmed, and consider how you can protect yourself in those situations.

Types of Boundaries:

- Physical Boundaries: These involve your personal space, physical privacy, and how much physical contact you are comfortable with.
  - Example: "I don't feel comfortable with hugs from colleagues. I'd prefer a handshake or verbal greeting."
- Emotional Boundaries: These define your emotional needs, including how much emotional support you can give or receive, and what emotional demands are acceptable.
  - Example: "I need time to process my feelings before discussing this. I'll be ready to talk tomorrow."
- Time Boundaries: These involve protecting your time and ensuring that others respect your schedule, commitments, and the time you need for yourself.

- Example: "I can't stay late today. I need to leave at 5 p.m. for personal reasons."

- Intellectual Boundaries: These pertain to your beliefs, opinions, and ideas. Intellectual boundaries protect your right to have different perspectives without feeling attacked or belittled.

  - Example: "I respect your opinion, but I see things differently, and I'd appreciate if we could discuss this calmly without insults."

2. Communicating Boundaries Clearly

Once you've identified your boundaries, the next step is to communicate them clearly and assertively. This means expressing your needs in a direct, respectful way, without apologizing or feeling guilty. Clear communication helps avoid misunderstandings and sets the stage for mutual respect.

How to Communicate Boundaries:

- Be Direct and Specific: Vague statements can lead to confusion, so be as specific as possible when setting a boundary.
  - Example: Instead of saying, "I need more space," say, "I need at least 30 minutes of alone time after work to decompress."
- Use "I" Statements: "I" statements allow you to express your needs without sounding accusatory or aggressive. They focus on your feelings and needs rather than blaming the other person.
  - Example: "I feel overwhelmed when I'm asked to do last-minute tasks. I need at least a day's notice for additional projects."
- Stay Calm and Confident: It's normal to feel nervous when setting boundaries, but try to stay calm and confident in your delivery. Avoid raising your voice, getting defensive, or apologizing for your needs.

- Example: "I understand that this is important to you, but I'm not able to help right now. Let's find another solution."

3. Enforcing Boundaries Consistently

Setting boundaries is only effective if you follow through by enforcing them consistently. This can be challenging, especially when dealing with individuals who are used to overstepping your limits. However, consistency is key to maintaining your boundaries and teaching others to respect them.

Techniques for Enforcing Boundaries:

- Be Firm but Polite: When someone oversteps a boundary, calmly and firmly remind them of your limit. You don't need to apologize or justify your decision—simply restate your boundary and stick to it.

- Example: "As I mentioned earlier, I'm not available to work after 6 p.m. I'll address this tomorrow during business hours."

- Use Consequences When Necessary: If someone repeatedly violates your boundaries, it may be necessary to implement consequences. This could mean distancing yourself from the person or limiting your interactions with them.

  - Example: "I've already told you that I can't lend you money. If you keep asking, I'll have to stop discussing finances with you altogether."

- Follow Through on Your Boundaries: Once you've set a boundary, it's essential to follow through consistently. If you give in to pressure or allow someone to overstep, they may not take your boundaries seriously in the future.

  - Example: If you've set a boundary about not taking work calls after hours, don't answer calls or texts during that time, even if you feel guilty.

4. Practicing Self-Compassion

Setting boundaries can sometimes feel uncomfortable, especially if you're worried about upsetting others or being perceived as selfish. However, it's important to practice self-compassion and remind yourself that setting boundaries is a form of self-care. You have the right to prioritize your own well-being, and it's not selfish to protect your time, energy, and emotional health.

How to Practice Self-Compassion:

- Acknowledge Your Needs: Recognize that your needs are just as important as anyone else's, and you deserve to have them respected.
- Let Go of Guilt: It's natural to feel guilty when setting boundaries, especially if you're not used to advocating for yourself. However, remind yourself that setting boundaries is necessary for healthy relationships and personal well-being.

- Celebrate Your Progress: Setting boundaries takes practice and courage. Celebrate each time you successfully set and enforce a boundary, even if it feels uncomfortable at first.

How to Deal with Pushback and Boundary Violators

It's not uncommon to face resistance when setting boundaries, especially from individuals who are used to overstepping them. Some people may react with frustration, guilt-tripping, or manipulation in an attempt to get you to back down. Dealing with pushback can be challenging, but it's important to stay firm in your boundaries and recognize when someone is violating them.

1. Understanding Why People Push Back

When you set boundaries, some people may react negatively because they're not used to you asserting your needs. Others may push back because they're manipulative or controlling and don't want to lose the power they have over you. Understanding why people resist boundaries can help you navigate their reactions more effectively.

Reasons People Push Back:

- Fear of Losing Control: Manipulative individuals may push back because they fear losing control over you. By respecting your boundaries, they lose their ability to influence your decisions or behavior.
  - Example: "You've never said no to me before. What's changed?"
- Guilt and Emotional Manipulation: Some people may use guilt to make you feel bad about setting boundaries, especially if they've relied on you to meet their needs in the past.
  - Example: "I can't believe you'd say no. I thought you cared about me."
- Inability to Respect Boundaries: Some people simply don't understand the concept of boundaries or feel entitled to your time and

energy. They may push back because they don't see why your boundaries should apply to them.

- Example: "Why are you being so difficult? I'm just asking for a little help."

2. How to Respond to Pushback

When faced with pushback, it's important to stay calm, assertive, and consistent in enforcing your boundaries. You don't need to explain yourself repeatedly or give in to emotional pressure. Instead, focus on restating your boundary and standing firm in your decision.

Techniques for Handling Pushback:

- Restate Your Boundary: When someone pushes back, calmly restate your boundary without getting defensive or emotional.

- Example: "I understand that this is important to you, but I've already explained that I'm not available on weekends. I can help you during the week if you still need assistance."

- Use "Broken Record" Technique: The "broken record" technique involves calmly repeating your boundary each time the other person tries to push back. This reinforces your limit without getting drawn into a debate.

  - Example: "I'm not able to do that right now." (When they continue to ask, repeat the same phrase.) "I'm not able to do that right now."

- Avoid Justifying or Apologizing: You don't owe anyone an apology for setting a boundary, and you don't need to justify your decision. Simply state your boundary and move on.

  - Example: Instead of saying, "I'm sorry, but I really can't help," say, "I'm not able to help with that."

3. Dealing with Persistent Boundary Violators

Some individuals will continue to violate your boundaries despite your repeated efforts to enforce them. In these cases, it's important to take more decisive action to protect yourself from further manipulation or overreach. This may involve limiting contact with the boundary violator, setting firmer consequences, or even cutting ties if necessary.

Strategies for Dealing with Persistent Boundary Violators:

- Limit Contact: If someone repeatedly disrespects your boundaries, it may be necessary to limit your contact with them. This could mean avoiding unnecessary interactions or reducing the amount of time you spend with them.
  - Example: "Since you've continued to ignore my request for personal space, I need to take a step back from our interactions."

- Set Firm Consequences: Consequences help reinforce your boundaries and signal that you're serious about enforcing them. These consequences should be proportionate to the violation and clearly communicated.

  - Example: "If you keep showing up at my house unannounced, I'll have to stop answering the door when you come over."

- Consider Cutting Ties: In extreme cases where someone consistently violates your boundaries and shows no respect for your needs, you may need to consider cutting ties with them. This is often a last resort, but it may be necessary for your emotional and mental well-being.

  - Example: "I've asked you multiple times to respect my boundaries, and you've refused. I need to end this relationship for my own well-being."

4. When Boundaries Are Tested in High-Stakes Situations

High-stakes situations, such as workplace dynamics, family conflicts, or romantic relationships, can make setting boundaries particularly challenging. In these scenarios, boundary violators may use more intense tactics—such as gaslighting, guilt-tripping, or power plays—to test your limits. Staying firm in these situations requires confidence and a commitment to protecting your well-being, even when it's difficult.

How to Stay Firm in High-Stakes Situations:

- Prepare in Advance: If you anticipate a challenging situation, prepare your boundaries ahead of time. Think about what you're willing to tolerate and what consequences you'll enforce if your boundaries are violated.
  - Example: "If my boss pressures me to work overtime again, I'll calmly explain

that I'm not available outside of my scheduled hours."

- Stay Calm Under Pressure: In high-stakes situations, emotions can run high, making it harder to enforce boundaries. Practice staying calm and grounded by using deep breathing or mindfulness techniques to manage stress.

- Seek Support: High-stakes situations can be overwhelming, so it's important to seek support from trusted friends, family members, or a therapist. Having a support system can help you stay firm in your boundaries and navigate difficult conversations.

  - Example: "I'm feeling pressured by my family to attend every event, but I need to set limits. Can we talk through some strategies for setting boundaries without causing too much conflict?"

Conclusion

Setting boundaries is one of the most powerful ways to protect yourself from manipulation and maintain control over your emotional, mental, and physical well-being. Boundaries define what is acceptable in your relationships, ensuring that your needs are respected and that others do not overstep their limits. By identifying your boundaries, communicating them clearly, and enforcing them consistently, you create a framework for healthier, more balanced relationships.

Dealing with pushback from boundary violators can be challenging, but it's essential to stand firm in your decisions and protect your boundaries from being eroded. Whether in personal relationships, the workplace, or social interactions, boundaries are the foundation of mutual respect and personal empowerment

Conclusion

In Don't Get Played: Your Guide to Outsmarting Manipulators, we have explored the intricate dynamics of manipulation, equipping you with the knowledge and tools to recognize and defend yourself against it in everyday life. The core themes of the book revolve around understanding the psychology of manipulation, building resilience through emotional intelligence and self-awareness, and asserting boundaries to maintain personal autonomy.

At the heart of manipulation lies the ability to influence others through subtle tactics like emotional manipulation, gaslighting, and coercion. Recognizing these tactics early is crucial in protecting your mental and emotional well-being. Key red flags, such as emotional blackmail, deceit, and undue influence, help you identify manipulative behavior before it takes control of your decisions.

Building resilience is the next step in defending yourself. Through emotional intelligence, self-awareness, and stress management, you can maintain clarity and composure even when faced with manipulative tactics. By learning to regulate your emotions, trust your instincts, and apply logic, you become less vulnerable to manipulation and more empowered in your personal and professional relationships.

Setting and enforcing boundaries is essential for protecting your autonomy and well-being. Boundaries prevent emotional burnout, foster healthy relationships, and act as a barrier against those who seek to control or exploit you. Enforcing these boundaries with confidence and consistency, while dealing with pushback assertively, ensures that others respect your limits.

Ultimately, this book provides the tools to navigate manipulation with confidence. By understanding the psychology behind manipulative behaviors, developing emotional resilience, and setting firm boundaries, you can protect yourself, maintain your independence, and foster healthier, more balanced relationships in all areas of life.

www.ingramcontent.com/pod-product-compliance
Lightning Source LLC
Chambersburg PA
CBHW061759250726
48657CB00001B/204